NOURISHING THE SENSES

Restaurant Architecture of Bentel & Bentel

Edited by John Morris Dixon

VISUAL PROFILE BOOKS INC., NEW YORK

Library of Congress Cataloging in Publication Data:
Nourishing the Senses: Restaurant Architecture of
Bentel and Bentel
Authors: Bentel, Carol Rusche
          Bentel, Paul
          Bentel, Peter

ISBN 13: 978-0-9975489-0-7
ISBN 10: 0-9975489-0-8

Distributors to the trade in the United States and Canada
NATIONAL BOOK NETWORK, INC.
15200 NBN Way
Blue Ridge Summit, PA 17214
Toll Free (U.S.): 800-462-6420
Phone (Outside U.S.): 717-794-3800
Toll Free Fax (U.S.): 800-338-4550
Email orders or Inquires: customercare@nbnbooks.com

Editor: John Morris Dixon
Designer: Martina Parisi-Nadel

Printed and bound in China

Contents

Foreword

American restaurants and their architecture have changed a lot since 1990 when Danny Meyer asked us to modify a service station at his Union Square Café. In the following years, young restaurateurs in New York City, as in other major metropolitan areas, opened fine dining places with an emphasis on quality and value in service and cuisine rather than obeisance to a grand tradition. These new restaurants were rooted in their locales by virtue of their service to local patrons, their use of regionally sourced food, their connections to neighborhoods, and their association with emerging culinary and restaurant cultures of their cities. Places such as Union Square Café gained increasing prominence, critical acclaim and, most important, popularity.

This was a change we experienced firsthand as restaurant patrons. But it was not until we had the opportunity to design such spaces that we became fully aware of the implications for their design. Change that was advantageous for the dining public turned out to be equally so for us, since it was consistent with our goals for our work. Contemporary, communal, regional, and artisanal were — and still are — hallmarks of our architecture. To the rising sensibility of up-and-coming purveyors of hospitality we brought our own passions for identification with place, material authenticity, craft, simple forms, and a compositional aesthetic that unifies every feature of a project, from the largest scale to the smallest.

Physical architecture is not the only salient feature of restaurants. Nor are restaurants only about the food or the service. Rather, they are about a broader experience of hospitality, that form of personal and professional conduct that binds all aspects of a restaurant together, from hello to goodbye and everything in between. Through our work, we have come to understand the relationship between all the elements that together constitute a great restaurant and our contribution as architects. The architectural quality of restaurants resides in the careful composition of essential components, carefully orchestrated and tuned to support the social activity of "dining out" and the cultural practices associated with preparing, serving, and enjoying food.

Our initial sense of what makes a dining experience special was not forged out of a reaction against the restaurant world that existed before. Instead we derived it from our personal family culture. Whether by birth or marriage, we are the children of architects trained as modernists and the grandchildren of craftspeople, many of whom were foreign-born and non-native English speakers. So we were twice estranged from popular culture — first, out of the respect for the avant-garde we acquired from our parents and second, out of the insularity of our family's foreign ways. These distinctions made our dining table exceptionally important as the centerpiece of daily life as well as ceremonial events. We took heart in cooking and eating together, drinking wine (generally homemade), gathering to discuss, argue and laugh together. The centrality of that custom to our lives informed everything we did then and still do today when we design restaurants. Not infrequently do we enter restaurants and absorb the sights and smells only to be reminded of a childhood experience in one or another of our extended family's kitchens.

But restaurants cannot — and should not — duplicate domestic environments or private customs. They operate in the public domain as purveyors of hospitality to diverse communities. We have learned much in the ensuing years about the professional commitments of those who envision and operate restaurants today: How to greet the guest, what makes a good table, what light best enhances the dining experience, where pressure points exist in the front-of-house, back-of-house and places in between, and how to facilitate different styles of service. Since no two restaurants are the same, the answers to these questions cannot be universalized. Thankfully, there is no science of restaurant design. Rather, great restaurants are the product of good judgment informed by knowledge, experience, conceptual clarity and, above all else, the burning desire to ensure there are no bad seats. We have been fortunate to work alongside the best in the business, having both given and taken lessons about what makes a great restaurant.

From these experiences — our participation in the development of a new breed of urban restaurants, our backgrounds and aspirations as architects, our personal histories and collaboration with others who have thought seriously about hospitality and worked in the field — we have acquired a broader sense of what architectural potential lies within the design of restaurants. We firmly believe that every act of building is materially and socially consequential. As with other building types that serve the public, restaurants are crucibles for the social practices that unfold within them. They are linked to the communities they serve both outwardly, as communal institutions, and inwardly, as environments of social exchange. If their architecture possesses significance at all it is because their form, space, and materials sustain those practices and nourish the human experiences that occur there.

This book provides the opportunity to look back at some of our recent work and to consider it as parts of a whole. Rather than compiling an encyclopedia, we have gathered together projects that offer variations on the central tenets of our work and give you, the reader, an opportunity to see how those variations play out in ever greater variety. For us, this is a look backward as well as a springboard for our future efforts, a chance to reflect on what we have been able to accomplish — in collaboration with all of our clients and colleagues — within this important moment in the evolving story of the American Restaurant and to challenge ourselves to continue to move forward along a trajectory of design it suggests.

We would like to thank all of those with whom we have had the privilege to work on the projects assembled in this book including: Bobby Baldwin, David and Michael Barry, George Biel, Frank Castagna, John Ceriale, Tom Colicchio, Paula and James Crown, Patrick Donelly, Katie and Paul Grieco, Will Guidara, Garrett Harker, Daniel Humm, Maguy LeCoze, Gregory Long, Glenn Lowry, Barbara Lynch, Joel Marcus, Danny Meyer, Gillis and George Poll, Gordon Ramsay, Eric Ripert, Aldo Sohm and Emmanuel Verstraeten; and those we have collaborated with, including Matt Adams, Michael Anthony, Jeremy Bearman, Andy Bennett, Marco Canora, Floyd Cardoz, Angela Hartnett, Kerry Hefernan, Tomo Kobayashi, Gabriel Kreuther, Chris Lanzisera, Pascaline Lepeltier, David Mancini, Mark Maynard-Parisi, Sisha Ortuzar, Terry Riley, David Swinghammer, Dean T. Kyle Vanderlick and Jean-Georges Vongerichten. We especially want to thank our dedicated staff without whose vigilance and commitment these projects would not have been realized with the quality they possess. We thank our immediate families for their support, assistance, guidance and the wonderful experiences that are the well-spring of our creative content. We dedicate this book to Maria and Frederick Bentel, the founding partners of Bentel & Bentel whose commitment to family and work continue to inspire our own love and passion for what we do. Their spirit lives on.

Introduction

Architects designing restaurants design objects as small as a spoon, as intimate as two chairs and table and as large and public as a banquet room for hundreds. This range reflects the special nature of the restaurant program. Simultaneously places of work and leisure, restaurants cater to the quotidian and the special event. Organized internally around their service, they connect with regional resources for food supplies, staff and cultural relevancy. While processing tons of raw food and dispersing waste, restaurants support the most refined and acculturated social practices. The contrasts evident in the program of a restaurant are not black and white, but rather finely graded. Between big and small, intimate and public, formal and informal, unprocessed and fully finished, there is a spectrum of things to design. Like nesting eggs, the spoon sits on the table served by the chair within the room of a building that is itself located in the city that draws upon a region. Restaurant architecture reflects that layered complexity.

The design of restaurants is at once an exercise in differentiation — the segregation of program parts by function, space needs and character — and one of synthesis as we and the cohort of owners, restaurateurs, and chefs, as well as engineers, equipment designers and restaurant personnel strive to achieve a unity of concept and execution. As architects of restaurants, we dwell on the particular and local, seeking threads of information about the place and purpose of the restaurant with the expectation that they will reappear, woven into the fabric of the design. We investigate, analyze, reflect, propose, test, prototype, reflect again, re-propose and compose with all of the artistic imperatives of achieving a composition that is more than the sum of the parts. That is why our work is varied, each project bound to a specific time and place but linked by a common method of inquiry and resolution of use, material, technique, light, form and space.

Restaurants, especially the urban restaurants that are primarily the subject of our work, are also social venues, places where communities of people gather. Restaurants not only serve their dining patrons. They can also anchor the communities around them as parts of a civic landscape, as neighborhood landmarks as well as rooted business enterprises and places of employment. Urban anthropologists recognize this attribute of restaurants when they interpret dining establishments of all stripes — the historical taverns, inns, bars of the past, as well as the diners, coffee shops, pizzerias of today and all of the cultural, ethnic, regional and national permutations of the restaurant — as the markers of urban neighborhoods. Evidence of this is provided by the most successful restaurants in New York City, including the "destination" restaurants that succeed because they are loved by locals as well as newcomers and outsiders.

Further evidence of the integration of restaurants into their locales is given by the diversity of successful restaurants by location within and among cities. We note the all-important differences of character and culture between restaurants in Brooklyn and Manhattan as well as in San Francisco, Chicago and Boston or Amsterdam, London and Beijing. This is as true of the one-off restaurants we have designed such as Cielo in Boca Raton and Island Creek Oyster Bar in Boston as it is of branded restaurants such as Houston's, Bluesmoke or the several Craft Restaurants. What passes in one place will not in another.

As with any creative effort, designing a restaurant is a process that passes through distinct phases from the initial conception and development to final execution. We are struck by the parallels between our work as architects designing restaurants and the work of our peers in the culinary arts who first plot their menus in response to the seasonal availability of their raw material and who transform that material through the application of their expertise and aesthetic sensibility. As with any design practice, the medium defines the way an audience will relate to it. In preparing and sharing food, chefs and restaurateurs provide physical and emotional satisfaction. As molders of man-made environments, architects form places that subsequently contain and influence the human activities taking place there. Architects conceive forms and spaces through an unfolding quest to locate a consequential vision in material form. As an introduction to our work we offer brief reflections on that vision as it is evident in our work.

Place-making

Places are memorable spaces, environments whose image we associate with an event or practice and that stimulate both visual and emotional recollection. As locations simultaneously of social and private engagement, restaurants are predisposed to conjure powerful memories, if not solely because of their physical features then because of the environment in concert with the food, the service, the company and conversation. The architecture of restaurants does not provide the content of these various components of experience, but rather supports them, constituting what some have called a "thick" space, one which performs discretely in response to the various needs of servers and those served.

For this reason, as designers we look first to the many overlapping uses of restaurant architecture. Guests arrive, dine and depart. Raw material comes in, is processed and is delivered as food or sent out as waste. These two intersecting arcs of activity underlie the restaurant program. Our design work begins with the orchestration of spaces that service them independently and in unison. This sounds like a rudimentary task and, indeed, it can proceed from a simple diagram of relationships of uses. But this mapping not only distributes parts of the program, it also clarifies the relationship

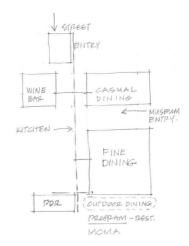

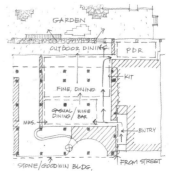

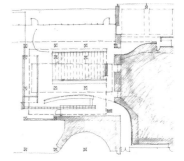

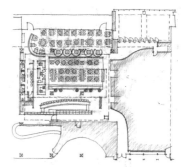

Figure 1 A,B,C,D: The Modern: Design evolution from Program Diagram to Plan Diagram, Ceiling Diagram to Seating Plan

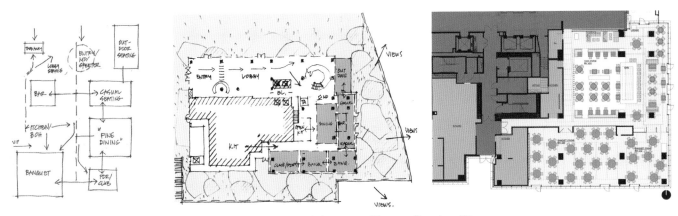

Figure 2 A,B,C: Riverpark: From Program Diagram to Schematic Plan to Seating Diagram

of the parts and suggests the final form of the plan (Figures 1 A,B,C,D; 2 A,B,C). The relationships we sketch out at the beginning of a project remain clearly delineated in the finished work, an important point that references the need to deliver a space that supports the hospitality concept. One sees this in the allocation of dining and service areas, the careful location of service points, the subtle but important distinctions between casual seating areas and fine dining locations. Notice also the clear route of entry at restaurants such as the Modern and Rouge Tomate which links the front entrance directly to the host stand and gives diners subtle guidance, ensuring that the routine of "greeting" is honored (Figures 3 A,B; 4).

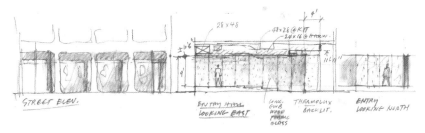

Figure 3A: The Modern: Schematic section through entry vestibule from street

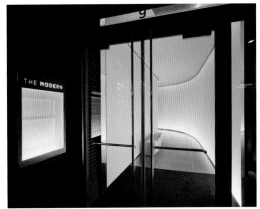

Figure 3B: The Modern: Entry view showing the elongated vestibule linking inside and outside

Figure 4: Rouge Tomate: View from entry door across bridge to greeter stand

The threshold between outside and inside is one that we try to establish clearly, since it marks not only the point at which the guest has arrived — and at which point the hospitality service commences — but also expresses a relationship between the restaurant and the neighborhood in which it is located. We find it difficult to ignore the physical or social context of a restaurant within a neighborhood. Look at the front room of Gramercy Tavern that opens both to the dining areas in the rear and to the street (Figures 5 A,B). This room takes the glassy storefront as its fourth wall. The engagement of the room and the public space of the street is reinforced by a three-sided art piece that relies on the open "public" side for its completion.

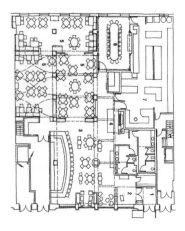

Figure 5A: Gramercy Tavern: Plan

Figure 5B: Gramercy Tavern: Bar area with its fourth wall on the street

We were inspired by its name to think that the architecture of Gramercy Tavern should embed the restaurant in its urban context. Tavern has its root in the French taverne or the Italian taverna, a place that provided travelers with food and shelter. The association with travelers links it to areas of the city where its services are most needed, along major thoroughfares, near ports, stations, streets, places where natives mingle with foreigners and where community identity is forged through the ancient social practice of hospitality. From its Latin root, taberna or "hut," tavern derives its flavor as a common part of the building environment rather than something monumental or exotic and set apart. A tavern is properly located adjacent to a public place where insider and outsider meet.

We recognized the subtle social messages restaurants convey again while working on The Modern, the restaurant at the Museum of Modern Art in New York City. It was one of our first restaurants located in New York Midtown business district. Through our prior work in the commercial districts of Lower Manhattan such as Gramercy Tavern and Craft, we came to appreciate the value of the plate glass storefronts to the character of our restaurants. The open façades — a historical artifact of the commercial storefronts that lined the streets of Ladies Mile — encouraged a visual connection to the passersby as we have seen at Gramercy Tavern. Midtown New York was different physically as a consequence of its genesis as a residential area later transformed into a business center. The street walls of Midtown Manhattan are generally closed visually, reflecting lesser reason for a connection between what happens on the street and what happens inside these buildings than in urban areas dominated by retail uses. This condition has become a hallmark of well-known Midtown restaurants that tend to be invisible to passersby. The Modern was destined for a space that was similarly segregated from the street by virtue of its location off the former Museum lobby. From the outset we wanted to create a distinct passageway with a recognizable architectural character that would draw visitors from the street. The arcing illuminated wall which you see in the final plan (Figure 1D) grew in importance as an organizing element for the whole space, defining the entry as well as the plan of the bar.

Place-making is as much about identifying a center as it is about marking a transition from one area within a space to others around it and when possible from inside to outside. Look closely again at the plan of Gramercy Tavern and you will notice plan elements that subtly break up the spaces without causing abrupt visual separations (Figure 6). We reinforce these connections with prominent markers using art as a focal point or a change in elevation that permits a view out over the adjoining spaces. (Figures 7 A,B,C).

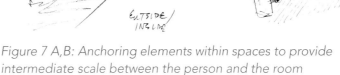

Figure 6: Gramercy Tavern: Openings between rooms differentiating spaces while permitting visual connections

Figure 7 A,B: Anchoring elements within spaces to provide intermediate scale between the person and the room

Figure 7C: Elevation changes establishing areas and views

These are more than spatial or formal gestures. The ability to see people elsewhere in the restaurant engaged in, for example, a casual drink at the bar or enjoying a complex multi-course meal, is central to our belief that this diversity enlivens everyone's experience. Yet, these visual interpenetrations should not intrude on any individual experience. Material changes, furniture placement, lighting, artwork to mark boundaries or to punctuate visual axes are devices that tangibly separate one space from another without the need to create spatial boxes.

Note also the careful arrangement of the dining rooms themselves. Our first instinct, one that is informed by the research we conduct wherever we travel, is that people feel comfortable when their location with respect to others is clearly defined. Our restaurants typically demonstrate a grouping of tables in ways that encourage the perception of a room as having a core and a perimeter, with three distinct layers of space across their width. We observed that the arrangement of interior spaces in thirds clarifies an individual's position in a room. The principle of three tables across is effectively a strategy of creating perimeter and center, polarities of experience that communicate their presence in spatial terms and that help the guests situate themselves physically and emotionally (Figures 8 A,B).

Materialization

While the plan gives structure and form to the architecture of restaurants, the three-dimensional development of the space — its materialization — is the means by which the spatial concepts embedded in the plan are fully realized (Figure 9). This is evident in all our work, but in particular in Craft, the first restaurant we completed for Tom Colicchio as an independent chef and restaurateur (Figure 10). Tom wanted to open a restaurant whose hallmark would be simple expert culinary execution: meats and vegetables prepared expertly in dishes distinctive according to the unique tastes of the ingredients. In his restaurant, Tom exercised his "craft" as the means by which raw material is transformed into a finished product.

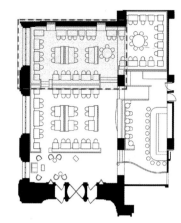
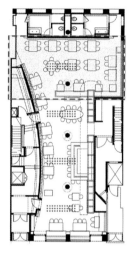

Figure 8 A,B: Plans of Eleven Madison Park and Craft showing three tables across the room

Figure 9: Materials reinforcing sense of place

Figure 10: Craft: Scale, texture, color, and density of materials reinforcing sense of place

Studying this, we strove for a suitable architectural expression and found it in a simple plan, lighting that supported the cadence of the room and the use of materials in ways that amplified their color and texture. In the same way that Tom selects food that is seasonally available or the product of a local artisan, we composed the surfaces in Craft from a palette of materials made available to us by talented craftspeople. The resulting composition renders bronze, leather, blackened steel, glass and wood as self-evident constituents of the space. We took advantage of the preexisting building fabric, a 19th-century retail and manufacturing building stripped of its ornamental detail by years of neglect, as a counterpoint to what we added as new. Rather than assigning a stylistic language to this material palette, we orchestrated the pieces according to their color, texture, scale, surface features, as well as the ways they are cut, tooled and finished.

Craft demonstrates that the architecture of building interiors is, perhaps more than the architecture of building exteriors, an exercise in the manipulation of space and then of surfaces, textures, color and light, often artificial, to further articulate those spaces. In the distinctions of one interior surface from another, our goal is not to create visual variety but rather to affirm the qualities of space that we have developed in plan. We place soft and acoustically absorbent materials next to diners, rough and textured ones where we have an opportunity for light to emphasize the quality of surface, dark where we need background for a visual feature, reflective where we seek a spatial expansion and light-transmitting to emphasize the texture and colors of the human face. The restaurant called Toku features textured slate on walls adorned with candles and lit from below, which serve as a welcoming gesture at the point of entry. Adjacent columns in the same textured surface march through the space and provide cadence and rhythm to the experience. Reflective ceiling planes identify the territory of the main dining area as distinct from the bar. Meanwhile, the banquettes are backed by acoustical material behind an uplit sheer fabric, dramatizing the seating niche, offering acoustical comfort to those seated in front and providing a color and texture that is complimentary to their faces.

Just as locally sourced food offers a tangible connection between a restaurant and the region it calls home, honoring local materials and working methods binds restaurant architecture to its locale. Craft has its terra cotta fire brick, a characteristic (but typically hidden) building material of its city. Reclaimed snow fence planks at Island Creek Oyster Bar recall the color palette of New England. Market by Jean-Georges at the W Boston Hotel features the local granite and cool hues of the waterfront. Craft LA carries forward the rich materials of the earlier Craft restaurants, but with a more essential treatment with less texture and more reflectivity to balance the interior with the directional sunlight of Southern California outside. North End Grill has its bracing palette of white porcelain and charred black wood inspired by oyster shell, fish scale and the black coal on which they are cooked. These are not stylistic references or visual graphics so much as they are spirited incarnations of a relevant local material culture.

The particularization of surfaces by material texture, color and character takes place on ceilings as well. Ceilings are the fifth elevation, a surface of importance both as backdrop to the elevations and as character-defining in itself. We have come to cherish the way a glossy ceiling plane such as that at The Modern picks up and reproduces the action taking place below, at the same time defining the territory of the room. As the lights dim and the contrast of the rough and smooth surfaces becomes more pronounced, the shiny surface becomes darker, picking up the color and light intensity of what is below it while the adjacent matte surfaces trap light and become luminous background for the dark floating plane. Through these subtle material differentiations and their related reactions to light, the lower ceiling plane opens up visually, conveying spatial infinity. The reflected movement of people and the flickering of light amplifies the inherent energy of the space.

The perimeters of the ceiling planes at The Modern, highlighted by their physical separation and their material distinction, also mark the limits of territories below and imply the thresholds between one area and another, allowing the viewers to position themselves in the restaurant and the Museum. As noted above, threshold is important to us as a device of place-making. At the Modern, changes in a floor material, the lowering of a ceiling, an important piece of furniture, the sudden but controlled opening-up of a vista are cues to a spatial transition from outside to inside and, once inside, from one area to another.

The acoustical properties of a space are no less an aspect of its material presence than stone, metal and glass and can work as effectively to support a larger design goal. Sound has an unquestionable impact on one's perception of space. To control it we recognize its source as energy and deploy materials for acoustical comfort as well as color and texture. This is evident in our use of acoustically porous wood fiber plank in the ceilings of restaurants such as Craft and Toku that deadens high-pitched sound while providing visual texture. Generally, we strive for 70 percent of the interior surfaces to be acoustically absorbent.

The potential for acoustically absorbent materials to tangibly influence our perception of space is given by the kitchen threshold at The Modern, a vomitory formed by canted walls that audibly disconnects one room from the other without a spatial barrier. To walk to the other side of the thick wall is to be transported across an invisible sound barrier that contains the back-of-house areas.

Articulation

For us, the articulation of physical features — of a material palette, through categories of objects, between dissimilar spaces — is nothing less than the developed expression of the design concepts governing place-making and materials. It is evident in the development of detail, the resolution of connections between parts as well as their precise juxtaposition, whether separated by a few inches or many feet. In some cases, the detailing is robust, as in the vigorous treatment of leather panels at Craft, where the texture, geometry and scale are counterpoints to the texture, geometry and scale of the historical fabric of terra cotta, brick and iron. In other cases, the detailing is highly refined and minimal as in the material terminations at Club 432 or Craft Los Angeles. In one case, fasteners are revealed, while in others elements are held together magically as though suspended in close proximity. Where exposed, fasteners introduce a finer scale and rhythm within a visual composition. Where hidden, their absence allows the viewer to experience the joining of materials as a synthesis rather than counterpoint, much like a slow reduction of flavors ultimately fused into a singular experience of the palate.

Le Bernardin provides an example of surface articulation and its role in defining an interior space. Maguy Le Coze and Eric Ripert wanted to reinvent this venerated restaurant without diminishing its special appeal. They surmised the younger audience that had learned from places such as Gramercy or Craft of a new, less formal dining style that still achieved excellence in food and service might never experience and appreciate the special virtues of their restaurant because of its formality. We responded by proposing casual dining in the bar area with a window open to the adjacent public way. But the restaurant had always had a discrete, internal orientation closed to view from the street. In order to achieve transparency to the exterior without sacrificing entirely the privacy with which the restaurant had been associated, we developed a metal screen consisting of flat bars 3" deep and 3/8" wide on their leading edge. Thinking of the screen in theatrical terms, as a scrim that when illuminated creates the visual illusion of opacity, we called for a matte finish on the opposing interior faces of the fins to trap light and to diminish the potential for distractions from activity outside. Then we polished the narrow face of the fins, causing them to work as a subtle mirror to the activities of the dining room (Figures 11 A,B). Lit from above and below, this fin wall permits the guests to experience activity outside subtly and without competition to the energy of the interior space and passersby to witness that which had previously been secluded.

Figure 11A: Le Bernardin: Concept for bar area with windows to the street shielded by aluminum screens

Figure 11B: Le Bernardin: Bar area with windows to the street shielded by aluminum screens

Further to reinforce the sense of relaxed comfort and engagement among the diners, we designed banquettes with slightly lower seat and table height (16" seat height and 26" table top height instead of the standard seat height or 18" paired with a 29" table top height), close spacing, a mixture of high and low dining heights, smaller tables and chair widths — all to encourage a more intimate and casual character for the space (Figure 12). The restaurateur has combined this with a service style that is less formal than in the adjacent dining room. In aggregate, the design of the place is forged from its physical features and service style to achieve a vigor augmenting the character of the restaurant as a place all its own. We repeated this exercise at Aldo Sohm Wine Bar to great success (Figure 13).

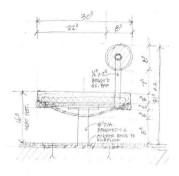

Figure 12: Le Bernardin, seating detail

Design articulation also pertains to the fit and finish of features of larger scale, things present in the design that enhance a systematic performance. Again, consider lighting: we regard its presence as being either ambient — to define general illumination of a space — focused — to create areas of foreground and attention as in a table top or a flower display — or accentuating surfaces, textures and colors (Figure 14). When light fixtures are present they act as architectural features, defining space through cadence or implicit scale. We conceived the glass walls of The Modern, the metal screens at Zylo or Le Bernardin, the wine rack at Cielo, the pendant fixtures at Colicchio & Sons, and the ceiling element at New York Central as both sculptural elements, architectural features that produce scale and rhythm, and light fixtures whose presence is marked by their luminous qualities (Figures 15 A,B; 16 A,B).

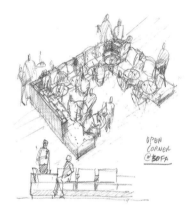

Figure 13: Aldo Sohm Wine Bar, seating detail

Figure 14: Light on walls to articulate material qualities

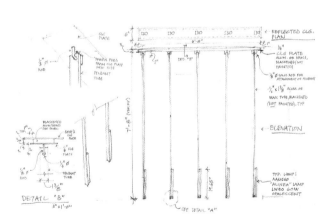

Figure 15A: Colicchio & Sons: Sketches for lighting

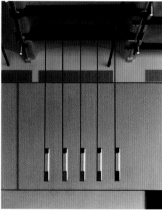

Figure 15B: Colicchio & Sons: light fixture

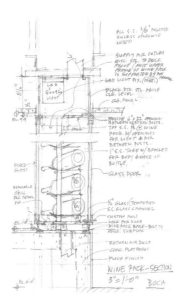

Figure 16A: Cielo: Sketch of illuminated wine rack

Figure 16B: Cielo, wine rack

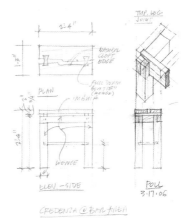

Figure 17: Toku: Details of furniture

Furniture — seats, tables, stools and those things that rattle when you shake the box — is another design element whose essential features articulate a design concept. We study the relationship between furniture and the space within which it sits. Dimension, color, texture of finish, physical support, weight and ease of movement are each discrete features of furniture that influence the diner's experience of a space. The bar stool at Le Bernardin whose seat is longer and narrower than typical in deference to the intimacy and casualness of the space, the large swivel stools at Big Bar that make it easy for a group to gather around, the tables at Craft that are longer and wider to accommodate multiple shared plates and the long banquette at The Modern, whose rolled back allows diners to drape an arm over its low crest and comfortably engage those seated in the adjacent room, are each elaborations of our ideas about how these spaces should work. Differences of fractions of an inch in seat height can dramatically change the way a patron engages the table top. Greeter stands, farm tables, wine displays and service stations play a similar role in informing character and supporting a design concept (Figure 17).

In our work, art pieces, whether flat or three-dimensional, moving or stationary, are integral to the design concept. Consider the Thomas Demand photograph at The Modern, the Stephen Hannock paintings at Craft and Eleven Madison Park, the Per Fronth glass print at Rouge Tomate, the Ran Ortner painting at Le Bernardin, the Robert Kushner painting at Gramercy Tavern and Kushner's mosaic at Tabla. In each case, the artwork is not present as a decorative object but as a part of the space, one of its many features, augmenting the restaurant's concept through its narrative and reinforcing the architectural content by affirming its territory and interconnections.

In these ways, with these instruments and this vision, we compose our spaces, linking disparate scales, rationalizing the relationships between distinct uses while accommodating their individual requirements, resolving formal and material intersections, orchestrating the palette in ways that enhance the sense of place as well as the physical comfort of those who use and experience these restaurants. As architects we embrace the differences of program and character and make that difference a subject of design. We commit ourselves to action followed by reflection and action again, a process and method through which we seek a refined and thorough result that fulfills the promise that we envision for architecture generally and, more specifically, for the architecture of restaurants.

We have worked with Bentel & Bentel on three major projects in the past seven years. They are **very good listeners** and **great collaborators.** They have been both **pragmatic and symbolic** in their designs because they draw from **a deep well of personal artistic creativity.** The result is **spectacular, timeless and evocative.** We, and our guests, are **nourished** when we inhabit their sculptural space.

David Mancini, General Manager, Le Bernardin, Prive, Aldo Sohm Wine Bar

"We wanted **avant-garde, modern,** but we wanted **timeless** too."

Emmanuel Verstraeten, Owner, Rouge Tomate

"The **passion** and **knowledge** behind everything they do is **nothing short of extraordinary.** Their work is much deeper than just creating something beautiful, but something that's **functional, timeless, and welcoming** to everyone that walks through the door."

Will Guidara, Owner, Eleven Madison Park

"We started with **luxury, contemporary, sexy, warm, and convivial.** Further on in the process, we added **sophisticated, serene, and comfortable.**"
Eric Ripert, Chef, Le Bernardin

"**Astute use** of new materials that **enliven but respect** the existing context."
Jury member for AIA Small Projects Award for Ground Café

"At last count we've worked with Bentel & Bentel on **eight beautiful restaurants,** including Gramercy Tavern, which was their very first foray into the world of hospitality. Each one of the projects is as **compellingly different from one another as night and day** — and therein lies the untold story on Bentel & Bentel. These are **collaborative listeners** of the highest order, and **they crave being challenged** to go places they have not yet been. They hear and tell stories via **flawless design, they sweat the details,** and in the end — they are happiest when they see **their creations come alive with happy people** providing and receiving hospitality in an environment that transports them to an even better place."

Danny Meyer, Restaurateur

"I want to **accommodate** everybody; this isn't an Austrian wine bar. It's not French. It's a New York **wine bar that represents different cultures."**

Aldo Sohm, Master Sommelier, Aldo Sohm Wine Bar

"We felt it was **crucial** that Gramercy Tavern's design be somewhat **universal** and **not too themed.** We wanted it to be **reminiscent** of an American Tavern, to suggest **without being overbearing."**

Danny Meyer, Restaurateur

"I just think that Bentel & Bentel has a **unique ability to combine an absolute understanding of every building** — from the historical standpoint to the material of the original design — where **every single line and detail matters** more and is more powerful than any massive, obvious display you see too much of today in restaurant architecture. It is an aesthetic of nuances, **distilling the best** of the historical benchmarks and the most visionary perspectives, **without ever forgetting** these places they build are to be lived and worked in, every day."

Pascaline Lepeltier, Master Sommelier, Rouge Tomate

"Walk past or drive past at 9pm and **the building** — an analogy for the entire city — **is alive.** Suddenly, as diners come and go from the hotel's Market restaurant, the theater district is given **a new vitality."**

John T O'Connor, in Esplanade magazine, on Market by Jean-Georges

"I think architecture, when it's functioning well, has the capacity to expand us and diminish us at the same time, to **create intimacy** in one moment and in the next to **take us outside ourselves.** As a New Yorker, moving from Gramercy Tavern to The Modern to Le Bernardin, what I'm struck by in Bentel & Bentel's work is a **sensitivity to the rhythm** of the human body. They build **walls that are not barriers,** but are **opportunities to experience the sensuality** of a surface, the **movement** of a plane, the **interactions** with the dynamic of interior volumes."

Ran Ortner, Artist of Le Bernardin painting, "Deep Water No. 1"

Le Bernardin

New York, New York

The redesign of the celebrated seafood restaurant met a need to update the entire space. One key objective of the owner was enlarging the lounge, which had been little more than a waiting area, making it a destination in itself, with a relaxed dress code and a casual menu. The words of chef Eric Ripert to describe this new vision: convivial, warm, sexy, and serene.

The first design decision was to retain the iconic teak ceiling, with major modifications to the lighting incorporated in it. Down-lighting now creates an essential pool of light on each table, complemented by up-lighting of surrounding surfaces to make the spaces seem less confined. The architects sought the effect of a glowing room in which patrons were immersed in an atmosphere of ambient light, offset by carefully orchestrated focal concentrations.

Everything below the ceiling is new. The architects reconfigured the former entry to gain a new window looking into the lounge from the adjoining through-block passage, plus a view outward to a featured sculpture there. In the lounge, new seating includes banquettes, a design choice inspired by the theme of conviviality. The curved bar increases the convivial feeling and was designed so that the chef could prepare some plates there, in view of patrons — providing an appealing touch of "theater." The tops of the bar and tables are onyx, and the maître d's stand is clad in this same translucent material. The bar's recessed front is surfaced with mother-of-pearl tiles.

Colors throughout the restaurant are drawn from nature and associated with the exquisitely prepared seafood served — tones of driftwood, sand, and water. Screens of teakwood blocks, placed as backdrops around the perimeter, establish a kinship with the ceilings and contrast subtly with the whites and off-whites in the foreground.

Scrims installed at the dining area windows, woven of fabric strips, dried vines, and metallic threads, modulate the view to the busy street outside and pick up light from the base of the wall. Screens of vertical, twisted aluminum strips with polished leading edges and a random brushed finish on their two broad faces, also up-lighted, produce a subtle shimmer. Where these occur along walls, they're backed by fabric-covered acoustically absorptive panels. The custom-designed carpet combines silvery grays and pale browns in a curvilinear pattern of "pools." Even the white onyx on some key surfaces includes subtle light brown veining.

The painting at the far end of the dining room, "Deep Water No. 1" by Ran Ortner, was not commissioned for the space, but was a fortuitous find, perfectly dimensioned for its position here. As in many spaces designed by Bentel & Bentel, this work of architectural scale creates a window, in effect, on a solid wall.

Restaurant location at corner of mid-block passage with LeWitt murals — entrance canopy at left

Early sketch of lounge with curved bar and art wall at rear of space

Lounge area with bar, architect-designed low seating, screen at windows of twisted aluminum strips

Bar area designed for conviviality, aluminum strips screening entry vestibule

Dining room under pre-existing teak ceiling complemented by new screen of teakwood blocks

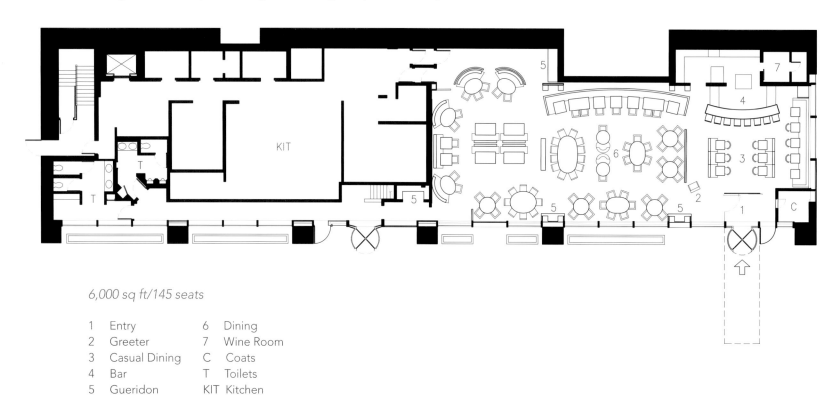

6,000 sq ft/145 seats

1	Entry	6	Dining
2	Greeter	7	Wine Room
3	Casual Dining	C	Coats
4	Bar	T	Toilets
5	Gueridon	KIT	Kitchen

Tables with curved banquettes, backed by teakwood screens

Details of screens — one of teakwood blocks, one of twisted aluminum strips, backed here by acoustic fabric

Architect-designed seating and handbag stand

Banquette backs that can form armrests

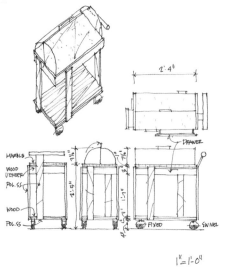

Cheese cart and architects' sketches for it

Painting "Deep Water No. 1" by Ran Ortner as backdrop for dining on seafood

Screen woven of fabric, vines, and metallic threads — uplighted — modulating view of street

Toku

Manhasset, New York

Toku is a rare demonstration of Bentel & Bentel's restaurant design skills in a suburban setting. It is situated on Long Island's affluent North Shore, in the Americana open-air shopping center, a locus of luxury shops that includes such internationally known retailers as Tiffany, Cartier, Hermes, Ralph Lauren, Prada, and Louis Vuitton. Offering a distinctive Pan-Asian menu, Toku meets a need at the Americana for a restaurant appealing to affluent daytime shoppers, while offering evening dining to residents of nearby communities.

Toku also presented the Bentels with an unusual opportunity to design a prominent front for the single-story structure housing it. The architects ingeniously capitalized on the fact that this façade faces north — thus getting virtually no sunlight — countering this lack by extending the front vertically with a tall light monitor. They faced this upper surface with striped translucent glass, which is back-lighted through clear glass behind it to produce a striking play of sunlight and shadow — replaced after sundown with lantern-like illumination.

While the Americana is no ordinary shopping environment, the space available for Toku presented the spatial constraints typical of restaurants located in rows of shops. Its footprint is narrow and, in this case, exceptionally deep. This tunnel-like expanse has been divided into a series of dining areas that flow seamlessly from the front to the rear without sacrificing the intimacy of each. An entry corridor, defined by bronze mesh curtains, leads patrons to a greeter desk just beyond the up-front bar. In the next area to the rear, a sushi bar lends its identity to a casual dining area. A more spacious dining area deeper into the space features a "lantern" of fabric hanging below a circular skylight, offering sunshine by day and a diffused overhead glow in the evening.

All lighting throughout is supplied indirectly from hidden sources — or by the wall-mounted candles first seen in the entry passage. Materials are limited to those of neutral blacks, whites, and earth tones. Porcelain-white stretched PVC panels on areas of the ceiling serve, as in several other restaurants by the firm, to mitigate the low ceiling height with soft reflections. Post-and-beam frames of ebonized oak — recalling historical East Asian architecture — delineate dining alcoves and an area at the far end of the space that can be closed off for private parties.

A few well-chosen works of art and craft underscore the identity of Toku's various zones. At the bar, up front, niches occupied by traditional paper lanterns alternate playfully with TV screens, and wooden monastery bells hang above the sushi bar. At the very end of the long space is a wood Buddha head seeming to levitate against the black slate rear wall.

Entrance front, with sun back-lighting glazed upper wall

Main dining area, with fabric "lantern" suspended under dome

1   Entry
2   Greeter
3   Casual Dining
4   Bar
5   Sushi Bar
6   Artwork
7   Dining
8   Private Dining Room
9   Buddha Head
10 Wooden Monastery Bells
11 Waiter Station
C   Coats
T   Toilets
KIT Kitchen

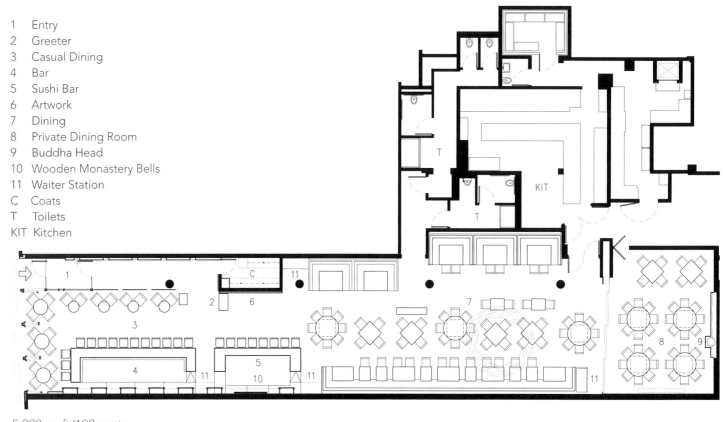

5,000 sq ft/190 seats

Entry passage between slate wall and bronze mesh curtain; onyx-topped bar, flat screens amid lanterns

Sushi bar, wooden temple bells above; ceiling panels of porcelain-white stretched PVC defining areas

Above and opposite: rearmost area that can be closed off for private dining

Booths set off by ebonized oak framing, with white leather banquettes

Ground Café – Yale

New Haven, Connecticut

Ground Café brightens a part of the Yale University campus that is well populated daily but had been lacking in public amenities. The new oasis is tucked into the ground floor of the Becton Center, a ruggedly handsome poured concrete structure designed by Marcel Breuer and completed in 1970 for the School of Engineering and Applied Sciences. Besides offering a convenient and congenial setting for coffee, pastries, and light meals, the café was intended to encourage interaction among faculty and students of the engineering school — along with those from other Yale departments.

In adapting a former seminar room on the building's street floor, the architects first expanded it by a third of its original area. The existing aluminum-framed glass wall that had been tucked behind the structural columns was replicated in an extension that gives the café visibility from the street, while still being sheltered under the overhang of the upper floors.

Inside the café, the architects did not entirely conceal the rough-textured cast-in-place concrete enclosure of the former seminar room, so integral to the architecture of the building. But they gave the space a richer, more intimate quality — and improved acoustics — by layering a palette of walnut planks and perforated aluminum sheets over its walls and ceiling, leaving some of the original textured concrete visible. The variegated bluestone floor had existed here — inside and out — and new stone was obtained from the original quarry for the room extension and a wainscot along one wall.

In a bolder move to enhance the cafe's appeal, the design incorporates a 23,000-diode LED "digital canvas" rising up one wall and across the ceiling, a display that is visible to passersby through the new glazed wall. The installation was inspired by the products of research going on in the Becton Center itself, which the architects found "not only computational, but visual — and beautifully so." The installation makes these digital images visible not just to students and staff of that building, but to the Yale community at large, "manifesting the connection between science and art."

Although the programmable LED device originated to display work of the engineering school's researchers, its administration soon agreed to make its programming available to the university's entire faculty and student body, underscoring the idea that the café was intended as a link between the school and the rest of Yale.

Café visible through new glazed extension

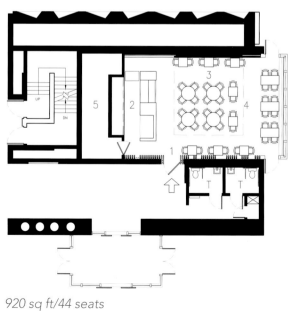

1   Entry
2   Service Counter
3   Café Seating
4   Digital Array at Wall and Ceiling Above
5   Pantry
T   Toilets

920 sq ft/44 seats

Bluestone paving extending inside and glass detailed like original building

LED "digital canvas" across ceiling and one wall

Digital display created either by building's engineers and scientists or by others at Yale

Wood screen revealing room's historic rough concrete wall and ceiling

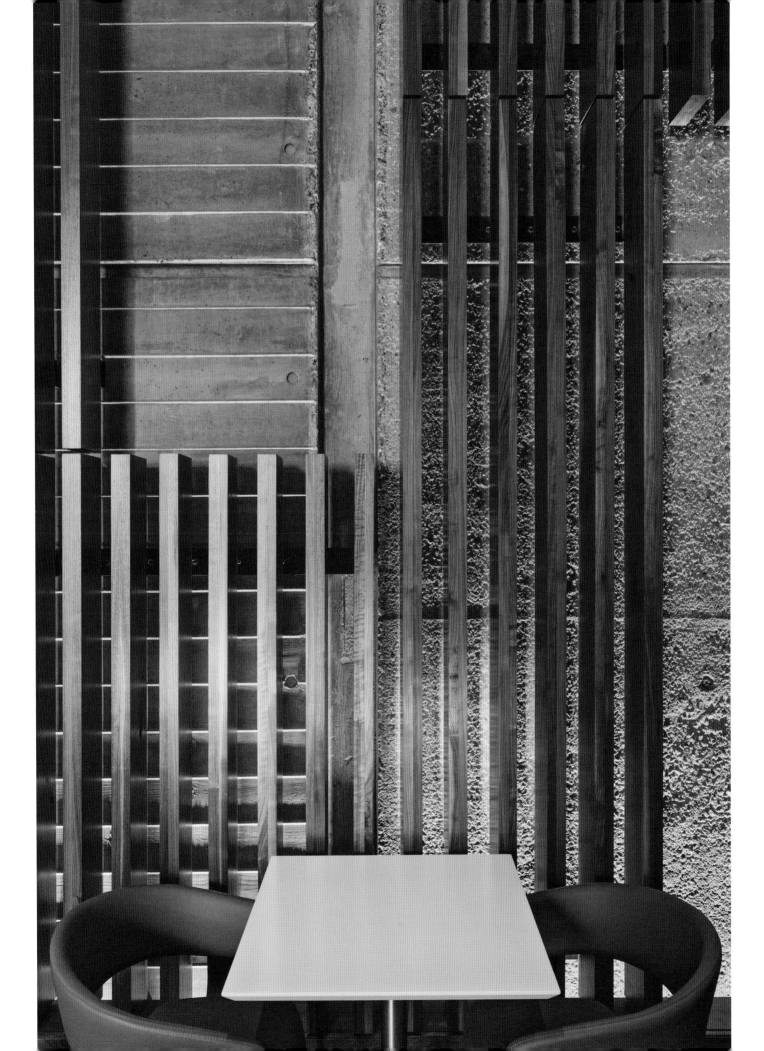

Eleven Madison Park

New York, New York

The imposing volume of a former banking hall now accommodates one of Manhattan's most celebrated restaurants. Eleven Madison Park occupies this space, at the base of a tower constructed for the Metropolitan Life Insurance Company in 1932 and listed in the National Register of Historic Places. Patrons enter the restaurant through one of the building's monumental arcades, which the AIA Guide to New York City calls "wondrous." Once inside, diners can view the abundant trees of Madison Square Park through tall, expansive windows.

Designing a restaurant for such a monumental space required balancing two conflicting objectives: exposing guests to its architectural impact yet placing them in comfortably scaled "communities" of tables. A key design decision here was to raise the floor level in the far portion of the room a few steps, thus creating two areas with more hospitable dimensions, but with a consistency of details and furnishings that avoids identifying either area as the favored place to dine.

The ornamented surfaces and hanging lanterns of the old bank have been scrupulously preserved. In order to provide appropriate lighting for evening dining, a series of hoops, with adjustable lamps, were suspended from the old lantern chains. After the restaurant had been opened for five years, when tax incentives for the room's preservation expired, they were replaced by a less visible system of downlights.

Notwithstanding the great room's impressive wall and ceiling ornament, the floors before the restaurant conversion were simply bare concrete. The architects designed new terrazzo flooring with angular patterns in muted colors that recall the angular forms of the tower above. The wood surfaces of the restaurant's cabinetwork and low partitions are ornamented with discrete geometrical patterns and images of the leaves of the ginkgo, linden, and sycamore trees in the centuries-old Madison Square Park outside.

The bar area in an adjoining low-ceiling area provides an intimate counterpoint to the lofty main dining room. Its totally new architectural treatment features a gold-leafed ceiling, with angular facets that refer to decorative motifs on the building's exterior. Deep-colored wood surfaces and elements such as traditional wall mirrors suggest the atmosphere of a brasserie. The mezzanine above the bar houses a private dining room that offers views across the main space to the park beyond.

Former insurance tower seen from park

Entry arcade looking toward restaurant entrance

Dining room in former banking hall, with officially protected original details, including hanging lights

"Before" photos showing original flooring and other features missing; early sketch, above, for renovation

Cabinetry embellished with leaf motifs related to park foliage seen in background

Among new elements, terrazzo flooring in Art Deco mode

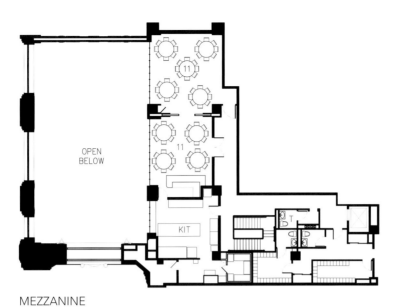

MEZZANINE

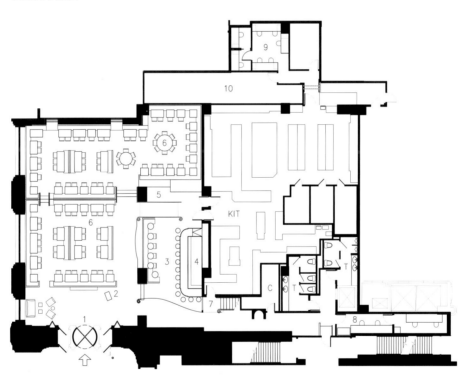

MAIN FLOOR

13,000 sq ft/298 seats

1   Entry
2   Greeter
3   Casual Dining
4   Bar
5   Beverage/Service
6   Dining
7   Stair to Upper Level
8   Reservations
9   Office
10 Wine Storage
11 Private Dining
C   Coats
T   Toilets
KIT Kitchen

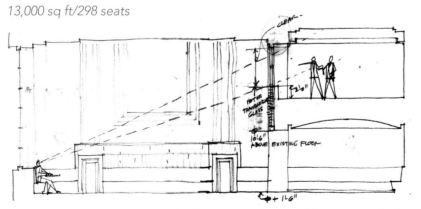

Section showing viewing angles from mezzanine and from patron below

Bar area with wood details recalling Art Deco

Band of historic Madison Square photos above seating

Tucked under mezzanine, bar area livened by faceted, gilded ceiling

Tabla

New York, New York

Developed at the same time as Eleven Madison Park, Tabla shares the same National Register building. But it was designed to be very different from its neighbor — more intimate, with a distinctive mission of "extending the idea of American food viewed through the kaleidoscope of Indian spices." In contrast to the relative design restraint of the larger restaurant next door, this one was intended to present a visual interpretation of those spices — evoking comparably intense emotional responses among diners.

The smaller scale of Tabla was enabled in large part because a 10-foot ceiling had been suspended in the original two-story-high space before National Register designation, so a second floor could be inserted to maintain that recorded first-floor height. Thus the concept developed for Tabla was to accommodate the bar and casual dining area on the street floor, with fine dining on the new floor above. That second level was treated essentially as a mezzanine, its floor plate pulled back from the enclosing walls in some areas to maintain the sense of a double-height space. This upper level is reached by a prominent stairway and overlooks the floor below through a central circular opening.

The architects specifically resisted literal references to Indian architecture, but did find inspiration in Indian mandalas, the diagrams that often guided that architecture. Specifically, the Vastu-Purusha mandala inscribes a human form — in the "perfect measure" seated position — within a square whose corners represent the four cardinal points of the earth. The abstracted depiction of the human in equilibrium with the pure geometry of the square encouraged the architects to emulate the profiles of the body — the curve of a thigh, the roll of a shoulder — within the rectangular volume to be occupied. These sensuous curves can be seen in the subtle cleavages between the mezzanine and the enclosing walls and in the cast-in-place, integrally colored concrete forms of the columns, the stairs, and the bar.

Some original Art Deco detail and ornament, having survived earlier alterations, has been retained and offers evidence of kinship with Eleven Madison Park. The intense colors of Tabla were inspired by Indian court miniature paintings of the 1600s, which display a particularly vivid green, along with distinctive yellows, whites, and reds — colors said to signify ardor as well as nature. The artist Robert Kushner, whose murals had enriched Gramercy Tavern, was commissioned for the stairwell painting here and the rotunda mosaics of vegetables featured in Indian cuisine, which were fabricated by Stephen Miotto.

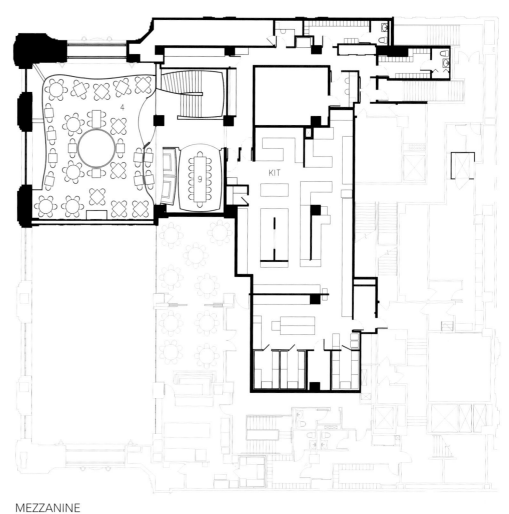

MEZZANINE

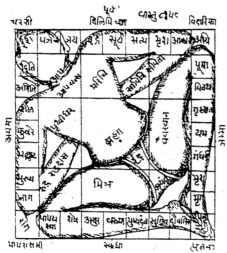

Mandala as design inspiration

1   Entry
2   Greeter
3   Waiting
4   Dining
5   Bar
6   Beverage/Service
7   Stair to Upper Level
8   Reservations
9   Private Dining Room
10 Bread Oven
C   Coats
T   Toilets
KIT Kitchen

10,500 sq ft/180 seats   MAIN FLOOR

Mezzanine-level dining room, semiprivate space with long table beyond

Street-level casual dining area with curved banquettes

Area under stair landing, with sculptural column

Stairs (above) to mezzanine (facing page) with painting and mosaics of flowers and vegetables by Robert Kushner

Market by Jean-Georges

Boston, Massachusetts

Situated at the base of a glass-enveloped tower in Boston's theater district, Market by Jean-Georges was conceived as a three-meal restaurant within the W Hotel. The restrained design of the restaurant itself reflects both the culinary philosophy of the chef and a New England ethic that prizes simplicity, directness, and the elegant orchestration of these qualities.

The restaurant space is blessed with two adjacent full-height glass walls, fronting on a prominent intersection, offering abundant natural light by day and merging at night into a luminous theater-street scene. Drapery with a carefully calibrated transparency captures enough light, day or night, to yield a subtle glow. The restaurant's signature design feature is a broad canopy of bleached oak, set against a darker background, lending the dining room a sense of enclosure while framing it when seen from outside in the manner of a proscenium. Suspended lighting fixtures discreetly lower the scale of this space for diners. Two ancillary dining alcoves are defined by vertically oriented screens in the same bleached oak.

The materials throughout have been chosen to evoke New England beaches, where nature and culture meet harmoniously — as they do in fine food preparation. The architects saw the combination of light woods against dark as comparable to that of driftwood, bleached on the surface and darker at the core. Mussel shells inspired the use of blackened steel and polished stainless. The bright white of the leather banquettes was seen as recalling sea foam, hovering above the earthy browns and grays of the porcelain tile floor. An adjacent private dining room displays the same materials and colors at a more intimate scale.

The restaurant's bar is not in the usual position, just inside the restaurant's entry, but placed at the far end of the space. Its location and intimacy separates it effectively from another bar adjoining the hotel's lobby. And it was designed to incorporate a raw shellfish bar, further distinguishing it as a regionally evocative destination for food as well as drink.

Location at base of glassy hotel tower (above and below) in Theater District

Dining room under bleached oak canopy, curtains modulating street view

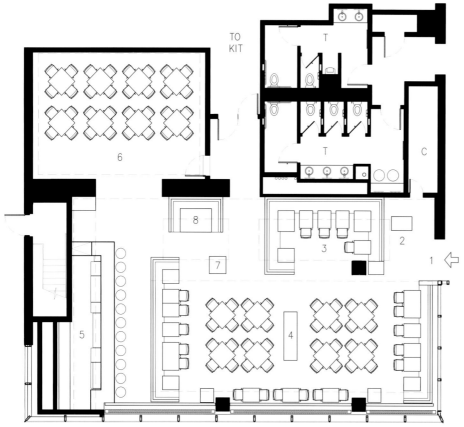

3,250 sq ft/127 seats

1   Entry
2   Greeter
3   Alcove Seating
4   Dining
5   Bar
6   Private Dining Room
7   Display Table
8   Chef's Table
C   Coats
T   Toilets
KIT Kitchen

TO KIT

Sketch section showing oak canopy over dining room

Bar at far end of dining room, offering shellfish as well as beverages

Rouge Tomate

New York, New York

In this restaurant, an innovative food concept that originated in Belgium was introduced to Midtown Manhattan. Like the original Rouge Tomate in Brussels, its first U.S. location was committed to the nutritional charter Sanitas Per Escam, or Health Through Food — a genuine respect for ingredients and the crafting of nutritionally balanced dishes. That commitment was expressed in the design's spare geometries, natural materials, and discreet displays of foliage and fresh produce.

The space the restaurant was to occupy presented both challenges and unusual opportunities. The clients had leased a two-story space — street floor and basement — formerly occupied by a women's fashion store. Located in an imposing early 1900s commercial building, it offered generous spaces and tall traditional windows on the street. The redesign retained some appealing features of the former store, notably the ample openings in the street floor, which allow patrons to perceive the entire two-story volume at once, and the dramatic stairwell that links the two levels.

Entering patrons cross a glass-railed footbridge to reach the greeter station, which is emblazoned with red squares evoking the Rouge Tomate logo and is set against a wall paneled with larger-scaled red rectangles. To one side, small plants are nestled in a screen woven of strips of white oak, a material integral to Rouge Tomate's image. Inserts of the signature white oak in the pre-existing walnut flooring delineate the restaurant's paths and areas.

The centerpiece of the street level lounge is the vividly red juice bar, its actual blenders contained in a glass cage to mute their sounds. A wall of back-lit white oak slats serves as the backdrop for this space and the dining room below it.

On the lower level, a similar wood-slat configuration partly screens the curved glass enclosure of the brightly lighted display kitchen. A wood-veneered ceiling contributes a warm glow to both the kitchen and the dining room. A ceiling-high triptych by the Norwegian artist Per Fronth depicting oak tree foliage generates the feeling of eating at a picnic table on a sunny day — and adds windows where none existed before.

At the opposite end of the dining area, the open stair from the upper level descends beside a shallow pool, in which float steel trays filled with cranberries that reiterate the Rouge Tomate red-squares motif. Projecting into this stairwell, adding to its dynamic atmosphere, are cantilevered dining booths, offering a special feeling of overlooking the restaurant's activity from a private observation post.

Street front with ample windows, red candles on sills

Entry across glass-railed bridge, signature red squares on greeter desk and wall behind

Seen from below, wall of woven white oak strips and fresh produce in square niches

Varied shades of signature red at entrance and in glass-enclosed blender center behind main-floor juice bar

Insets of white oak in pre-existing walnut creating distinctive floor pattern for main-floor dining area

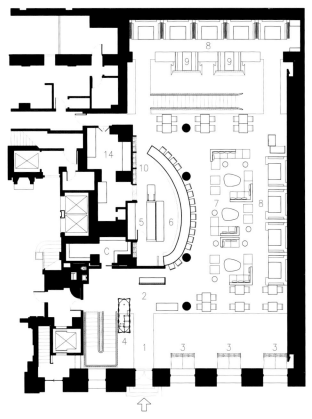

STREET FLOOR

1   Entry
2   Greeter
3   Two-story Artwork
4   Tomato Tower
5   Juice Room
6   Bar
7   Casual Dining
8   Dining
9   Balcony Booths
10   Wine Storage
11   Peninsula Booths
12   Private Dining Room
13   Cranberry Pool
14   Service Area
15   Display Kitchen
C   Coats
T   Toilets
KIT   Kitchen

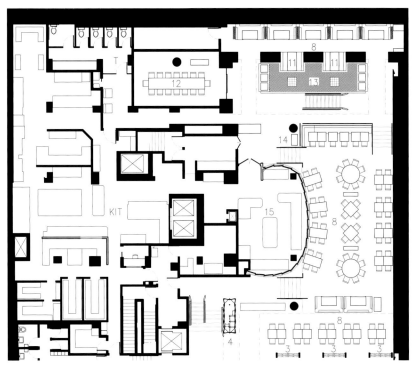

BASEMENT

17,500 sq ft/279 seats

Two-story wall of back-lit oak strips as backdrop for pool with floating trays of cranberries

Glass-encircled kitchen as focus of lower dining room

Visible from both levels, photo images of oak forest on glass panels by artist Per Fronth

In private dining room, wall of end-grain walnut blocks and live-edge table top

Houston's

Boston, Massachusetts

For the first location in New England for the widespread restaurant brand Houston's, this location was ideal. It is directly across a busy pedestrian thoroughfare from historic Faneuil Hall, in an area teeming with tourists and office workers. But the space the restaurant was to occupy — a cave-like volume under the elevated plaza of an office tower — presented exceptional design challenges.

Bentel & Bentel dealt with this situation in several creative ways. One key step was to design a forward extension of the space, which gives it greater visibility as well as additional square-footage. Taking cues from the area's severe masonry structures, some with bronze-capped domes or cupolas, Bentel & Bentel clad this extension — both walls and roof — in bronze. They then opened up its public face with an extensive glass front framed with a bold, simply detailed bronze "proscenium."

To further mitigate the cavern character of the interior, they opened glazed slits in the bronze roof and wall surfaces to admit shafts of daylight. Farther back in the space, they placed three tall, prismatic light monitors that pierce the office tower's paved plaza, serving as sculptural features there and welcoming daylight deeper in the restaurant. Another design move was to raise the floor of the space, as found, which was too tall a volume to fit Houston's well-established concept of intimacy. Elevating the floor level by several feet had the added benefits of bringing it closer to the pedestrian level outside and simplifying accessibility ramps.

The bronze of the exterior cladding was applied to some of the interior surfaces, as well, juxtaposed to the warmer textures and colors of woods and leathers. The simple, elementary geometries of the exterior give way inside to more intimately scaled configurations. The atmosphere of warmth thus produced is reinforced by the centrality of the kitchen, exposed both visually and environmentally to the patrons.

The relatively limited openings into the light monitors have been enhanced visually by expanding configurations of parallelograms around them, with the natural light illuminating their wood surfaces. At the rear of the restaurant, a potential feeling of confinement is eased with a stacked brick wall surface that suggests openings beyond it. In keeping with an established practice for Houston's restaurants (now re-named Hillstone's nationwide) the owners placed a notable artwork from their extensive collection just inside the entrance: a cast bronze horse sculpture by Deborah Butterfield.

Front of below-plaza restaurant framed by bronze "proscenium"

Design drawing showing daylight slots in extension's bronze roof and light monitors on plaza

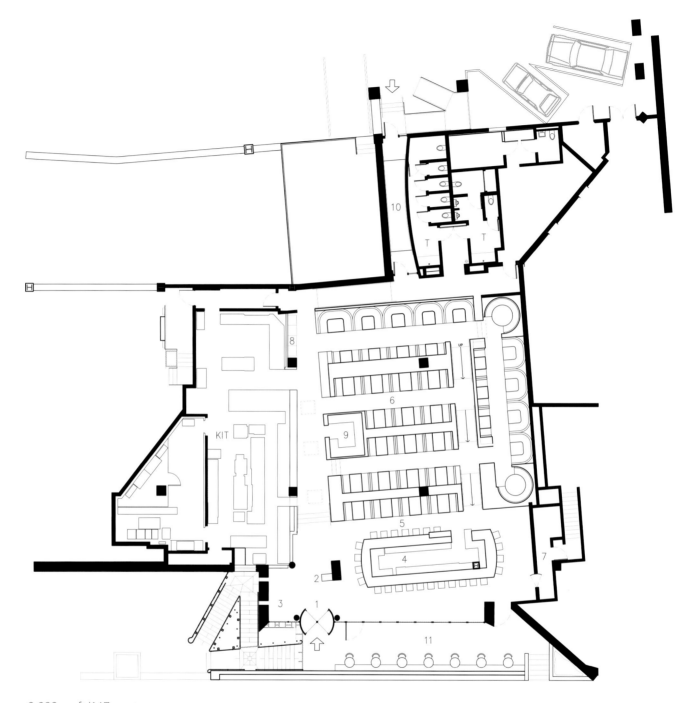

8,000 sq ft/167 seats

1	Entry	8	Wine Display
2	Greeter	9	Beverage/Service
3	Sculpture	10	Rear Entry
4	Bar	11	Outdoor Seating
5	Bar-height Booths	T	Toilets
6	Dining	KIT	Kitchen
7	Access to Lower Office/Coats		

Island bar just inside glazed front and under canopy of wood beams

Back wall of stacked brick implying opening to space beyond

After dark, light monitors illuminated from restaurant below

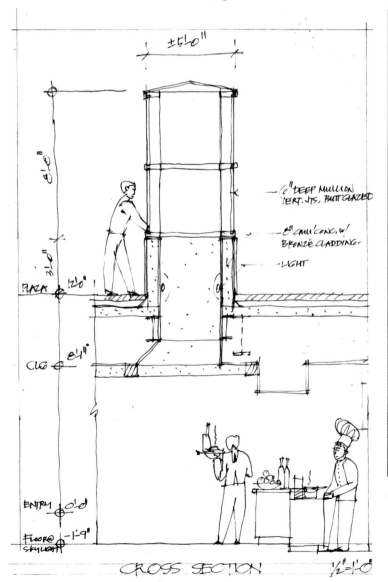

CROSS SECTION   ½"=1'0"

6" DEEP MULLION
VERT. JTS. BUTT GLAZED

8" CMU CONC. w/
BRONZE CLADDING.

LIGHT

±5'0"

8'0"

3'0"

PLAZA   1'0"

CLG   8'4"

ENTRY   0'0"

FLOOR @   -1'9"
SKYLIGHT

Light monitors seen against office tower

Inside restaurant, light from monitors dispersed over wood-clad surfaces

Aldo Sohm Wine Bar

New York, New York

Designed to convey the expertise and geniality of a well-regarded sommelier, this alternative to a full-scaled restaurant is located on a gracious through-block passage in Midtown Manhattan. Its bright canopy and entry vestibule are centered under a large-scaled mural by the renowned Sol LeWitt, a few doors away from Le Bernardin, which flanks one entrance to the passage.

The wine bar's interior is conceived as a "living room," occupying a single clearly defined rectangular volume. At its center is an extensive "sofa" with colorful pillows, wrapped around an area of low tables and black leather hassocks — all resting on the rectangle of a custom-designed rug. A ceiling-high wood screen on the axis of the entrance lends the space an effective sense of privacy from the world outside, while not actually obstructing the view in or out.

Lining the perimeter of the space are rows of bar-height chairs and tables. Centered at the end of the room is the "wine bar's" actual bar, which is freestanding, much like the island counters in contemporary kitchens. With this homelike arrangement, there is no firm spatial distinction between servers and those they serve.

Shelves along the room's walls show objects that Sohm has collected, much as personal mementos would be displayed at home. A variety of artworks commissioned for the space — characterized by bright colors and playful compositions — are organized in groups on the walls. The use of various woods, dark and light, contribute to the domestic feeling. Crafted light globes suspended in the space form a kind of canopy, lending a desired sense of intimacy to the tall volume.

Opening from one corner of the main space is a small-scaled wine-tasting room, with seats around a dining table of residential dimensions. This room has its own palette of muted colors, and on its walls are small-scaled, sepia-toned photographs of vineyards, which can be changed, depending on the wine of the day.

Aldo Sohm Wine Bar's setting along mid-block passage through an office complex

Entrance centered under Sol LeWitt mural

Just inside entrance, view of central "sofa" on axis behind wood screen

Feeling of "living room" within a tall volume

Also Sohm serving at freestanding residential-style bar

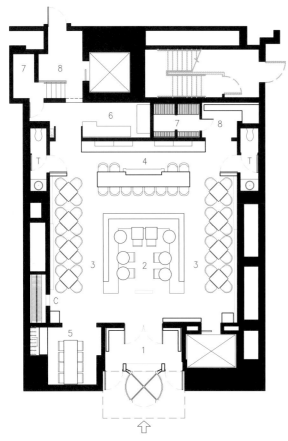

2,000 sq ft/68 seats

1	Entry	6	Pantry
2	Lounge Area	7	Storage
3	Bar-height Tables	8	Service
4	Bar	C	Coats
5	Tasting Room	T	Toilets

Central sofa area, under "canopy" of suspended light globes, surrounded by taller seats at high tables and bar

The Modern

New York, New York

While the overall design of the Museum of Modern Art's 2004 expansion was by Yoshio Taniguchi, the museum tapped the recognized talents of Danny Meyer to operate the museum's greatly expanded food services and of Bentel & Bentel to design them — a collaboration that had been notably successful at restaurants such as Gramercy Tavern and Eleven Madison Park.

The largest of the museum's new dining places, The Modern, is located on the first floor, with its own street entrance, so that it can function beyond museum hours and be a destination in itself. Its 322 seats are clearly divided between an ample area for the bar plus a casual dining area and a discreetly separated fine dining space, with a different menu. There is also a private dining room for special functions seating up to 64 (divisible into two equal rooms).

For Bentel & Bentel, the commission presented a rich combination of opportunities and challenges. The major asset of the restaurant's allotted space was the view of the museum's celebrated sculpture garden through a 75-foot-long glass wall, and this outlook became a signature feature of the fine dining portion. Challenges included guiding arriving guests through narrow entrance corridors, either from the street or from the museum interior. And there was the further challenge of building within disparate structural systems and ceiling heights dating from three periods in the museum's evolution: its original 1939 building, a 1951 addition, and a swatch of the new 2004 construction. The earlier portions have low ceilings for such expansive floor areas, while a higher ceiling in the recent addition lends dignity to the fine dining area.

It was considered essential to maintain a design kinship with the museum as a whole. Among its salient characteristics are: rectilinear forms, with occasionally radius-curved departures; flat white surfaces complemented by the muted sheen of glass and metal. The dark terrazzo flooring Taniguchi chose for the museum's main floor is extended into the restaurant, with areas of carpet or of hardwood like that of the art galleries distinguishing some areas.

In the bar and casual dining area, reflective panels of stretched PVC mitigate the effect of the low ceiling, and a panoramic photomural by artist Thomas Demand along the far wall helps convert a space that could have felt confined to one that seems both intimate and indefinite in extent. See-through wine racks separate the bar from the entry corridor from the museum. Translucent panels of sand-blasted glass partially enclose the fine dining zone.

The fine dining area has been laid out so that no seat faces directly away from the garden view. Sound-absorbing baffles are suspended from skylights in the high-ceiling portion of the space. Doors in the long glazed wall offer access to fair-weather seating on the terrace outside.

Preliminary sketch, showing restaurant in first floor of museum wing at left, overlooking sculpture garden

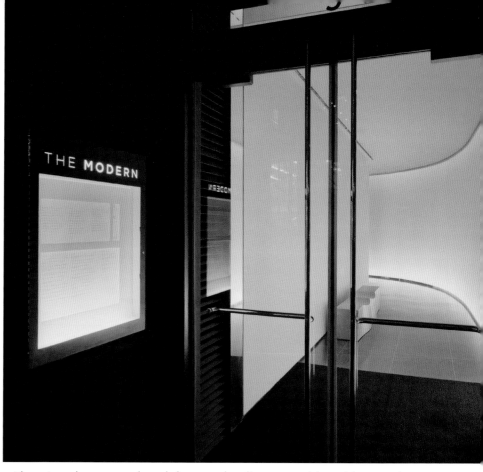

Restaurant street entrance, next to 1939 facade with restored canopy; glazed doorway leading to corridor with curved, back-lit wall

Corridor from the museum — to right of Sol LeWitt painting — separated from bar area by see-through wine rack casting shadow pattern on opposite wall

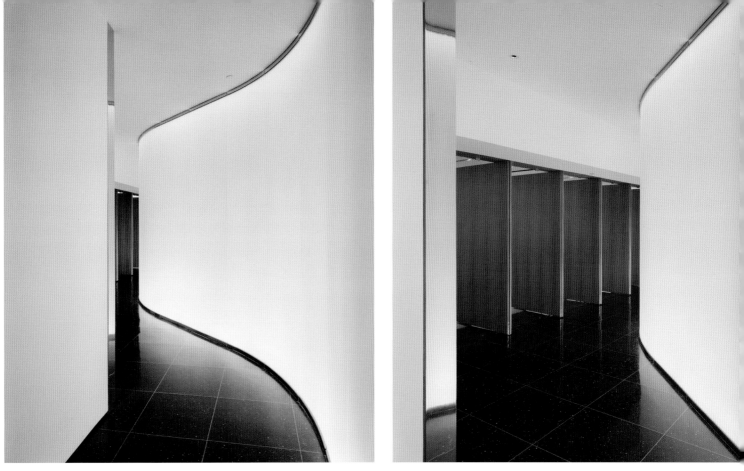

Passage to private dining room, with curved wall like that of entry corridor; pivoting wall panels of private dining room

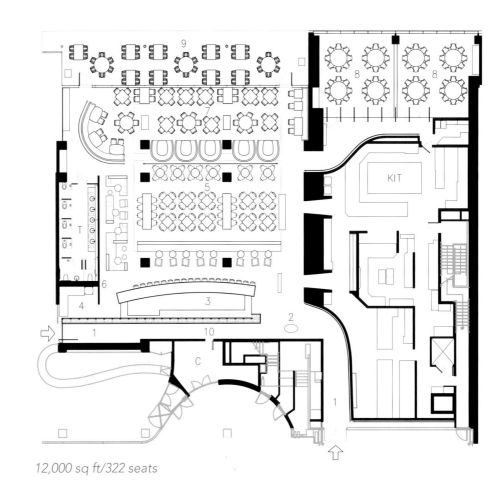

1   Entry
2   Greeter
3   Bar
4   Beverage Station
5   Casual Dining
6   Art Wall
7   Fine Dining
8   Private Dining
9   Outdoor Terrace
10 Wine Storage
C   Coats
T   Toilets
KIT Kitchen

12,000 sq ft/322 seats

Reflective ceiling panels and back-lit bar dissolving the confines of the room

Photographic mural by Thomas Demand on end wall and translucent panels partially closing off fine dining zone

Long black leather banquette separating immediate bar area from casual dining space, which has hardwood floor

Higher space along garden wall under skylights

Booths (right) under lower ceiling, facing garden

Left: unisex restroom, lavatory counter opposite toilet compartments
Above: service counter in niche
Right: Garden façade with dining terrace

Café 2 at MoMA

New York, New York

The Museum of Modern Art includes two restaurants designed by Bentel & Bentel and operated by the noted restaurateur Danny Meyer. On the first floor there is The Modern, the ample bar-dining and fine dining destination designed to function separately during and after museum hours. On the second floor, reached only through the museum and offering a sophisticated selection of light meals and beverages, is Café 2.

The space allocated to Café 2 is essentially one floor of the 1964 museum addition designed by Philip Johnson, a long narrow space with views to the street at one end and the museum garden at the other. In order to optimize the number of museum-goers who can be served, most of the seating is at long communal tables.

The "fast-casual" serving strategy applied here improves on the traditional cafeteria by eliminating meal trays and check-out lines, as well as the space-consuming pick-up stations. The time spent on line at the Café 2 entrance can be put to use choosing menu options from blackboard-style listings on a wall of the access corridor. From the head of the line, one is directed to a counter backed by an enticing view of cheeses and prosciutto in a walk-in refrigerator. After placing an order and paying there, the diner takes a number and chooses a seat anywhere in the room, where the order will be delivered. (Café 2 has recently tried a more traditional service, where staff members lead diners to tables and take their orders there — the wall menu still serving to speed up their selection. The restaurant design accommodates that system equally well.)

To serve the "community" of museum-goers, who may be seeking a respite from visual stimulation, most elements of Café 2 are simple in form and within a limited color range. The principal displays to be seen here are the foods in custom-designed glass cases — not unlike those that protect art objects in the galleries — and wine bottles in backlit perforated stainless steel tubes. The architects designed the tables in the manner of those in a monastery refectory, reflecting the shared devotion to art and ritual seriousness attached to museum-going.

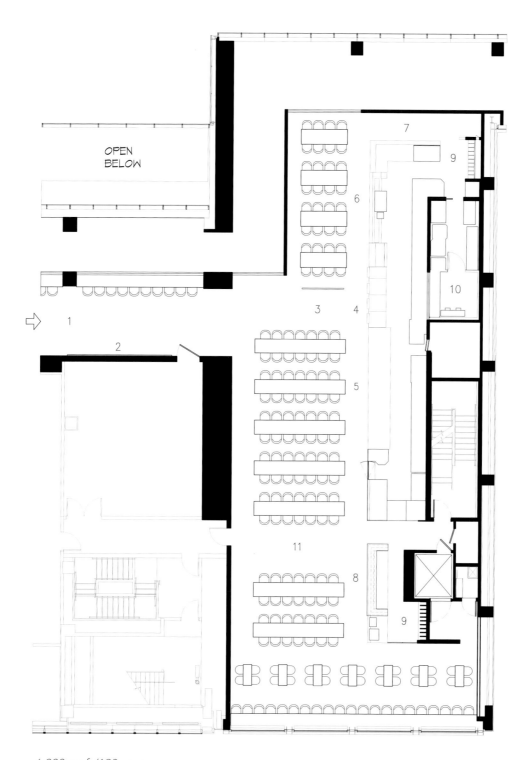

6,000 sq ft/190 seats

1	Entry	7	Coffee/Beverage
2	Menu Board	8	Beverage Service Station
3	Queue Area	9	Wine Display
4	Point of Sale	10	Refrigerated Display
5	Food Display	11	Casual Dining
6	Pastry & Dessert Display		

Refectory-style shared tables

Bar-height tables with mesh handbag or package racks

Counter seating at street-facing windows

Menu wall on approach to queuing area

Pastry and dessert display

Coffee and beverage counter

Display of menu offerings, with carefully calibrated angles and lighting

Café Vettro

Las Vegas, Nevada

Urban density arrived on the sprawling Las Vegas Strip with the construction of City Center. Included in this 67-acre, 18-million-square-foot development are four hotels, a condominium building, a shopping mall, a casino, a convention center, a dozen restaurants, and its own monorail. A major component of City Center is the 4,000-room Aria Resort and Casino, which includes the space that became Café Vettro.

While City Center, and the Aria Resort in particular, include outdoor areas serving as parks in this dense setting, these spaces provide only limited respite from the vast extent of enclosed space. The architects immediately recognized that the size and shape of the portion allocated for Café Vettro, with extensive exposure to natural light, offered an opportunity to create an airy, park-like clearing within the Aria's compressed interior.

They found design cues in the immense dimensions of the given space — 400 feet long and 35 feet high, offering 18,000 square feet at casino level with an added 8,000 on a mezzanine they would create — with a curved perimeter of curtain wall that admits copious daylight. The fact that the restaurant is approached from the relatively dark, inward-oriented casino inspired them to allude in their design to the natural world not far outside Las Vegas.

Arriving from the compression of the casino floor, the restaurant patron is not faced with a conventional door, but with an open passage toward a brighter space, recalling the way daylight plays on the region's ravines. This passage is framed on the left by a sheer concrete plaster wall and on the right by a tiered construction composed of locally collected rocks on blackened steel shelves, seen through sand-blasted glass and back-lighted. Within this opening, a 90-foot-long ramp slopes up toward the greeter's stand, where the full volume of the 560-seat restaurant is revealed.

The metaphor for the natural world is maintained throughout with abstract references to the forest. To divide the café's volume into more moderately scaled areas, the architects introduced the restaurant's most distinctive elements, its groupings of internally illuminated tree-like cones composed of stacked green glass discs. The massive concrete columns that march through the space are tinted brown, suggesting trunks of lofty trees.

The stairs to the mezzanine rise along the cliff of layered rocks that is seen at the entrance. At night, back lighting can make these masses look almost weightless. Supported on this stony construction is the natural-ledge-like edge of the mezzanine, under which is an arc of relatively secluded booths. A variety of ceiling surfaces and furnishings throughout the restaurant extend the palette of nature-inspired textures and colors.

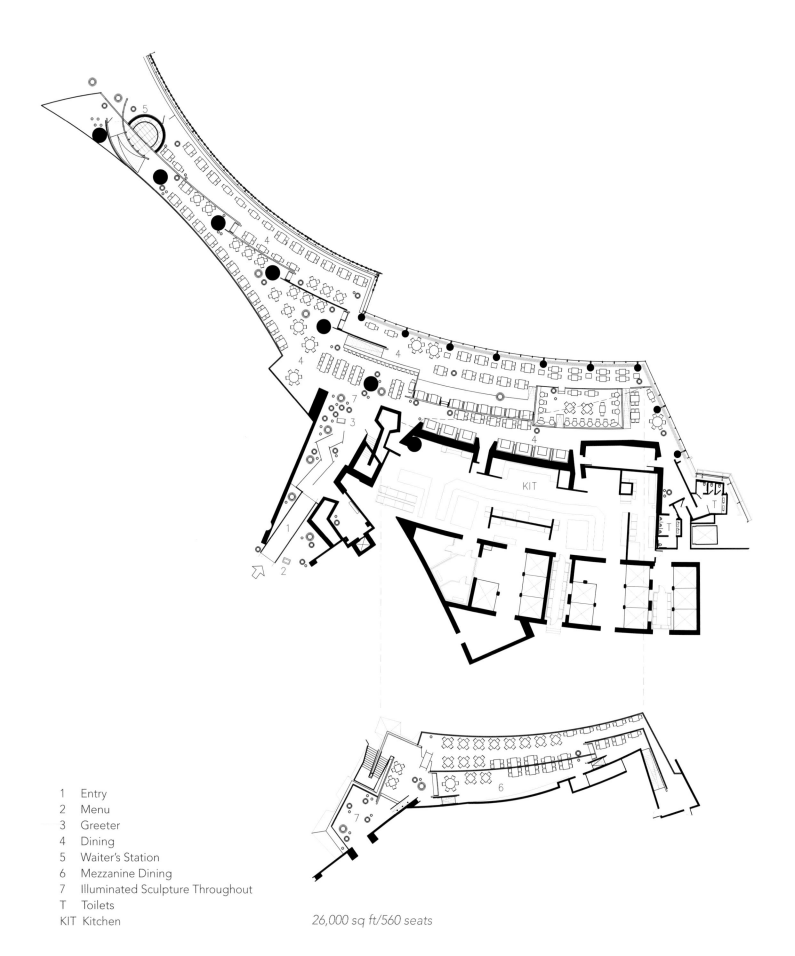

1 Entry
2 Menu
3 Greeter
4 Dining
5 Waiter's Station
6 Mezzanine Dining
7 Illuminated Sculpture Throughout
T Toilets
KIT Kitchen

26,000 sq ft/560 seats

The 35-foot-high space by day, with ample natural light through extensive glass walls

Café at night, with lighting from suspended luminous glass box fixtures and from plaza outside

Variety of seating and tables

Spaces punctuated by illuminated glass cones and massive concrete columns

Tiered walls of rocks under glass

Craft

New York, New York

Tom Colicchio, the chef for whom the architects designed this restaurant, believes that cooking of any kind is a craft, not an art. His culinary plan is to apply uncomplicated craftsmanship to explore the full flavor of each seasonal ingredient and to serve each food on a separate plate, centered on the table for all to share. Hence the name of this precedent-setting restaurant and its namesakes that he has since established — and the Bentel firm has designed — in other cities.

Taking a cue from his dedication to craft, Bentel & Bentel sought to create an architectural equivalent to his distinctive culinary approach. "Our goal," they write, "was to shape a simple yet texturally rich interior that reinforces his aspirations for food and service both functionally and metaphorically."

The space to be occupied was one of the characteristic 19th-century Lower Manhattan mercantile buildings being widely adapted for new uses. A generous 14 feet high, the restaurant extends back 80 feet from the street, but narrows to little more than 20 feet where essential service demands intrude on its 40-foot width.

Of the distinct design elements the architects cite as parallels to Colicchio's craft approach, the most prominent is the treatment of the structural columns that march through the center of the space. These have been stripped to the terracotta block cylinders laid up in the 1880s to fireproof the steel members within them. Facing each other across the narrowed center of the restaurant are a two-story wine vault, functionally framed in steel and bronze, and a curved wall of Brazilian walnut and leather panels with visible fasteners. Extending across the entire back wall is a commissioned triptych by Stephen Hannock, entitled "Squid Boats on the Gulf of Siam" and dealing principally with darkness and bursts of light. Arrays of suspended bare light bulbs serve as stripped-down "chandeliers" and modulate the loftiness of the space.

These distinctive elements help distinguish intimate "communities" of tables without shattering the refectory-like unity of the interior as a whole. And all of the restaurant's materials, fittings, and furnishings are installed without protective treatments, encouraging natural variations in texture and color as they age. In both its dining concept and its design, Craft has proven to age as gracefully as its time-tested architectural materials.

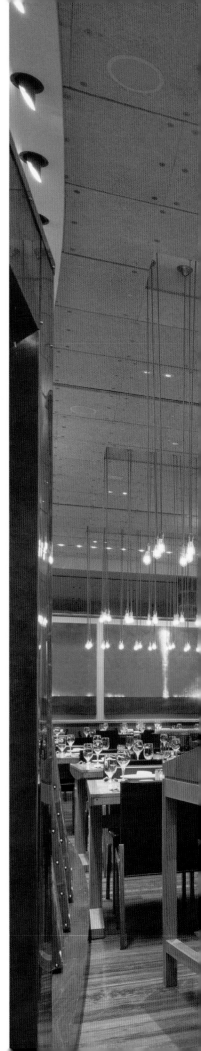

Street front of 19th-century mercantile building

Bar, wine rack catwalk above, looking toward rear of restaurant

View toward street with curved leather-clad wall to right

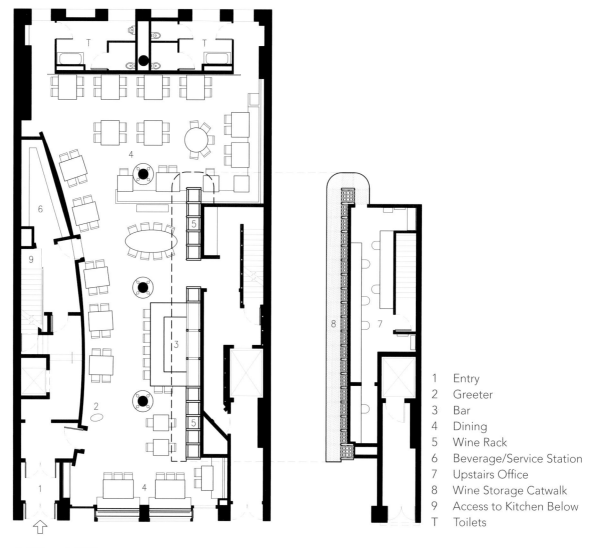

1   Entry
2   Greeter
3   Bar
4   Dining
5   Wine Rack
6   Beverage/Service Station
7   Upstairs Office
8   Wine Storage Catwalk
9   Access to Kitchen Below
T   Toilets

4,400 sq ft/102 seats

Concept sketch of space, curved wall to left

View from wine rack catwalk, showing columns, curved wall, and Stephen Hannock painting on back wall

Detail of leather-clad wall with visible fasteners

Detail of wine storage with mesh slings

Exposed structural brick on side wall of rear of dining area

Suspended lights and custom-designed table

End of wine rack catwalk over dining table

Cylindrical column, to be signature feature of later Craft restaurants, here with old fireproofing tile exposed

Craft Los Angeles

Los Angeles, California

In this fourth of the six Craft restaurants Bentel & Bentel designed for chef Tom Colicchio, they again used a limited set of materials and the simplest craftsmanship to relate the architecture to his approach to cooking. Here, as elsewhere, he applies the highest form of uncomplicated craft to explore the full flavor of each farm-raised ingredient and serves each one unadorned on its separate plate, to be shared by all at the table.

The parameters of the plan here specified a total of 275 seats, including a 40-seat private dining room and a 75-seat outdoor terrace, supported by a 3,500-square-foot kitchen and a 1,000-bottle wine case. Their design approach, here as elsewhere, drew on the specific context, which in Los Angeles was radically different from the 19th-century urban fabric of the original Craft in New York. Here, the restaurant occupies a new one-story aluminum-and-glass building, with a terrace overlooking a lushly planted park at the center of the recently refurbished Century City office and cultural superblock.

The building's muscularly curved floor-to-ceiling glass wall overlooks the terrace and dominates the interior. Responding to the sinuous plan of this wall, the architects rotated its curve vertically to form continuous fabric-covered panels that swath the ceiling and one wall of the main dining room. Two straight vertical planes set perpendicular to each other — a standing-seam bronze partition and a blackened steel and glass wine case — help define the major interior program areas of bar, main dining, and private dining rooms.

The building's columns, clad in sandblasted bronze plate, punctuate the patrons' experience throughout the restaurant, while recalling the hefty columns in the original New York Craft and its namesakes in other cities. The sensual appreciation of these materials is heightened by their contrasts: taut fabric-clad panels against roughened bronze column surfaces, the crisp transparency of the wine rack balanced by the old-growth oak flooring and custom-designed teak and walnut millwork used both inside and outside.

Throughout, all furnishings and fittings were designed by the architects to celebrate their materials and the elegantly simple craftsmanship of assembling them. These materials are intentionally left unprotected to encourage variations in texture and color that will be induced by age and use.

Craftsmanship underscored with bronze column and wall surfaces, oak floors, walnut table tops

Bar with illuminated glass base and down-lighted back-bar shelves

Main dining area with taut-fabric wall and ceiling surface, recessed bands of lighting

Booths subtly separated by bronze wire mesh curtains

Dining area backdrop of wine racks behind glass

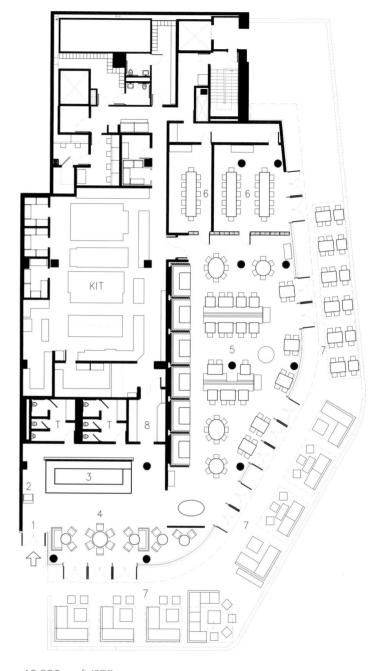

13,900 sq ft/275 seats

1	Entry	6	Private Dining Room
2	Greeter	7	Outdoor Dining
3	Bar	8	Beverage Service
4	Casual Dining	T	Toilets
5	Dining	KIT	Kitchen

Bold cylindrical column common to Craft restaurants, here clad in sand-blasted bronze

Outdoor dining in curtained shelters

Similar materials and emphasis on craftsmanship indoors and out

Craft Atlanta

Atlanta, Georgia

The restaurant's location in a two-story modified Neoclassical structure, situated among the brash high-rises of Atlanta's Buckhead district, suggested a demure though direct response by the architects. And within this building, Tom Colicchio's straightforward approach to fine cooking — exploring the full flavor of each ingredient on his seasonal menus — inspired the architects to design with a limited set of materials, using the simplest and best craftsmanship to assemble them. Their goal was a texturally rich interior with a generosity of space that evoked Southern design traditions while simultaneously expressing the restraint of the chef's approach to food preparation.

Entering from an automobile court shielded from the intense traffic of Peachtree Road, guests first encounter a wood-fired grill clad in copper and steel, which not only emphasizes the craft of cooking but acts as a symbolic hearth for the two-story volume. Past the grill, the three-inch-thick solid walnut top of the bar provides a warm contrast to the blackened steel and glass wine vault that screens an intimate lounge beyond.

A grand staircase composed of continuous walnut planks rises to draw guests up to the second floor, the rooms of which overlook the activity of Peachtree Road and the courtyard of the tall hotel to which the restaurant is allied. The spatial compression and release of the several dining areas on the upper level provide varying degrees of intimacy while preserving the communal quality that the chef seeks in his restaurants.

The interweaving of a distinctive palette of materials on both floors — walnut, steel, copper, oak, brick, cherry, leather, and muslin — recalls the character of historic domestic interiors, but in a distinctly modern manner. All furnishings and fittings — including cherry dining tables, walnut banquettes and sofas, and steel hardware — have been designed to celebrate their materials and the simple craftsmanship of assembling them. The absence of any protective coating on these materials intentionally promotes their ability to age naturally with grace.

The restaurant design is pointedly related to the surrounding community and its key role in the identity of Atlanta. Its spaces are open to Peachtree Road on both first and second floors. Twelve-foot-high French doors on the street side of the casual bar area allow a direct visual and physical connection between the patrons inside and the activity outside. That ensures that the liveliness of the interior is immediately evident from the boulevard. This positive visual exchange improves the pedestrian experience of the district, which the City of Atlanta is actively seeking to promote.

Previous page, wood-fired grill just inside entrance. Above, entry area, stairway, casual dining beyond

1   Entry
2   Greeter
3   Display Kitchen
4   Bar
5   Casual Dining
6   Dining
7   Outdoor Dining
8   Beverage/ Service
T   Toilets
KIT Kitchen

SECOND FLOOR

FIRST FLOOR

8,200 sq ft/236 seats

Diversity of second-floor dining spaces

First-floor bar seen from foot of stairs

Second-floor dining area with generous windows and wood shutters

First-floor dining space with wine vault

Stairway with Stephen Hannock painting "Incendiary Nocturne"

Banquette seating at second-floor dining area

Cielo

Boca Raton, Florida

The Italian word "cielo" can mean both sky and heaven. It is an apt name for the "jewel-in-the-crown" at the Boca Raton Resort and Club, a North American showcase for the chefs Gordon Ramsay and Angela Hartnett. Located on the top floor of the resort's 27-story tower, the restaurant offers nearly 360-degree views of the ocean, the Intracoastal Waterway, and the Florida hinterland.

The full-floor space, previously occupied by another restaurant, was redesigned to take greater advantage of its lofty views. To this end, the architects raised the level of the 27th-floor elevator stop so they could create a two-level environment. Arriving guests, those at the bar and at platform-level tables, look outward across the lower dining spaces lining the near-continuous windows.

The ambiguous boundaries and predominant whites and blues of the restaurant reinforce the suggestion of both sky and heaven. Variously reflective and louvered ceilings make the spaces seem taller than their actual dimensions. The ceiling panels reflect light coming up from the ocean surface and reproduce some of its shimmer. In contrast to the white of ceilings, curtains, and furniture, the floors and walls are dark, muted blue, a hue that virtually disappears in juxtaposition to the panoramic views, both day and night. After dark, the ceilings reflect the light of candles at each table, creating the impression of a starry sky.

Along with its strong orientation to the views, the restaurant design organizes the components such as the bar, chef's table, and alcoves around the tower in such a way that these spaces are both separate and connected, giving the diners a sense of calming stasis and spatial fluidity. This is especially important in such a restaurant, where the experience of "community" is as important as the privacy of the individual diners.

With similar aspiration to render a sense of community and shared experience, the architects laid out the seating at the point of entry so that incoming patrons present themselves to the audience seated in the bar area. The human energy concentrated on the "proscenium" through which they pass is palpable. From this point — marked by a glowing onyx greeter station — guests promenade to the dining areas around the core, proceeding along the upper and lower tiers of seating. The wall-length artwork "Split Sky" by Per Fronth recapitulates the rippled reflections of the sea outside, making the experience even more celestial.

Historic resort's 27-story tower, crowned by restaurant

Passage from elevators to greeter's desk...

...over illuminated glass floor

Greeter's desk and bar area on upper tier, dining area and view beyond

Bar area, with reflective ceiling panels and fabric modulating skylight illumination

Banquette forming barrier between different levels

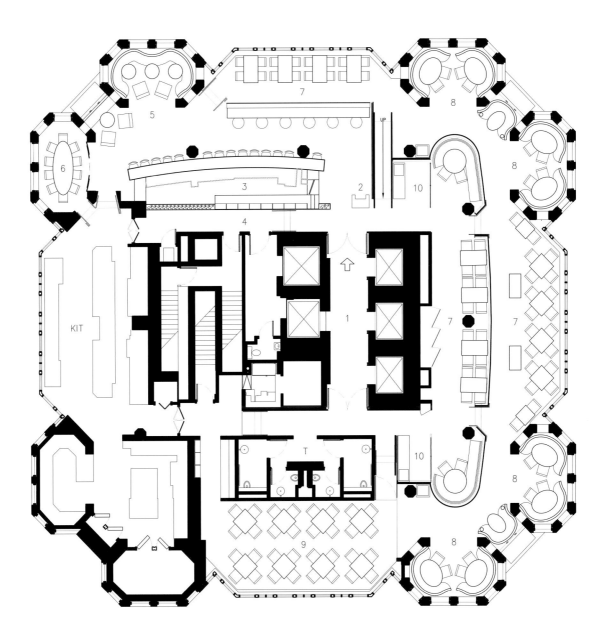

7,800 sq ft/170 seats

1 Entry
2 Greeter
3 Bar
4 Wine Display
5 Lounge Seating
6 Chef's Table
7 Dining
8 Dining Alcove
9 Private Dining Room
10 Service Station
T Toilets
KIT Kitchen

Curved termination to upper-tier seating

Two levels of seating, with art work "Split Sky" by Per Fronth — photo transfer on plexiglass — reflecting light and view

Area often devoted to private parties, with wall paneling designed by architects

Turret space accommodating chef's table

Turret seating for bar area (above) and dining (opposite)

Illuminated frosted glass at curved end of upper tier

Gramercy Tavern

New York, New York

The first all-new restaurant the Bentel firm designed for the trend-setting restaurateur Danny Meyer, Gramercy Tavern marries the genteel traditions of the Gramercy Park neighborhood with the owners' modern concepts of food and drink service. By taking the historic tavern as their inspiration, the architects have installed a series of architectural episodes within a gracefully aged industrial building, reconciling the apparent opposites of the rustic and the refined, the bucolic and the urbane.

The design also had to reconcile the extra-tall first story of its century-old structure with a need for intimate dining spaces. The ample volume was used to advantage in the bar area just inside the entrance, which is exposed to the street through tall glazing. The scale of the restaurant was then reduced toward the rear for the more intimate dining areas — none more than three tables across.

For some of these spaces, non-structural piers have been inserted between the building's widely spaced columns to establish the desired scale. In much of the restaurant, the tall ceilings are crossed by dark wood beams — also non-structural — moderating scale, adding texture, and helping to conceal necessities such as lighting, sprinklers, and air diffusers.

The Tavern's entire interior is firmly related to its stately old facade by extending the horizontal band of the transoms above its windows and doors throughout the interior. In the up-front bar area, this band is occupied by the mural "Cornucopia" by Robert Kushner, playfully representing fruits and vegetables. In the several distinct dining areas beyond, this same zone accommodates a series of arches and vaults.

Just inside the entry, the restaurant provides a welcome alcove of comfortable seating for those who may have to — or choose to — wait before proceeding to their tables. The tavern-like character of the bar area is underscored by the use of varied furniture, looking as if it were accumulated over a long period. An open wood grill at one corner of this area can offer patrons the sight and scents of actual cooking. The curve of the long bar itself is functionally effective for servers, while reinforcing the sense of conviviality among those seated there.

The rearmost portions of the restaurant, including its private dining room, extend into what was originally a lean-to addition to the building's first floor, with a low, sloping roof. Here, the architects reconfigured ceilings to peak over the rooms, recalling the interiors of rural outbuildings. In rooms such as these, one feels far removed from contemporary Manhattan while enjoying some of its most up-to-the-moment dining pleasures.

Restaurant interior seen through 19th-century commercial façade

Wood grill in corner of restaurant's front "tavern" area

Tavern seating, curved bar, and "Cornucopia" murals by Robert Kushner

The chalkboard reads:

TAVERN COCKTAILS
APROPOS
EXPAT
HOP TO IT
ORANGE BLOSSOM
RICKSHAW
MEZ CALIENTE
NORSEMAN
BACKHAND
SLOE STORM
TRISTAR SMASH

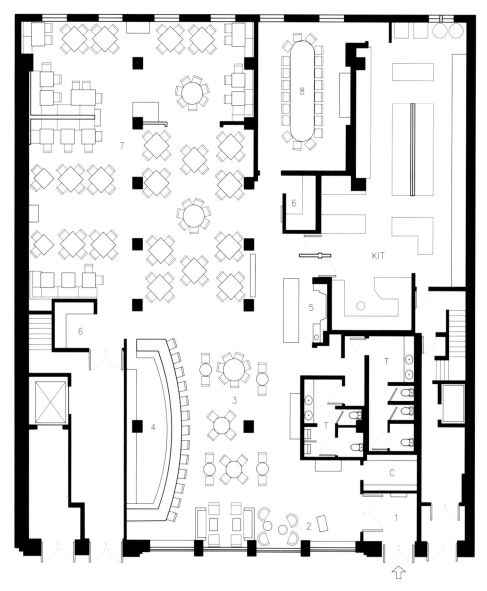

6,500 sq ft/196 seats

1   Entry
2   Greeter
3   Casual Dining
4   Bar
5   Wood Grill
6   Beverage/Service
7   Dining
8   Private Dining
C   Coats
T   Toilets
KIT Kitchen

Arched partitions with rough-hewn wood screens defining dining areas

Tavern '93

Vaulted and pitched wood ceilings giving two areas more intimate scale

Greater intimacy in private dining (above) and curtained alcove (opposite)

Riverpark

New York, New York

Situated in the new Alexandria Center for Life Sciences building within the equally new East River Science Park, Riverpark provides a culinary destination with spectacular river views in the largely restaurant-free Bellevue Hospital area of Manhattan. The design had to effectively serve the tenants of the building (pharmaceutical companies, healthcare-related start-up companies, and related firms) while appealing to the mix of residents and workers in the neighborhood. The goal was a welcoming series of both public and private dining spaces that would capitalize on the stunning views, with a bar/lounge accommodating 30, public dining for 120, private dining for 150, with the flexibility to combine all areas for parties of up to 300.

Since the restaurant was to be operated by the chef Tom Colicchio, the design also responds to the simplicity and directness that have been hallmarks of his food service. Accordingly, the architects chose durable and ageless materials such as bronze, limestone, cork, walnut, and oak.

While floor-to-ceiling windows along the eastern edge of the space allow patrons near them to enjoy the riverfront panorama, the depth of the space limits outward views for those seated farther inside. A raised platform at the center of the space both improves sight lines for those seated there and defines its own territory. To underscore the platform's central role, a bronze lattice dotted with crystalline lights is suspended above it, and its perimeter is delineated with fixed leather and walnut banquettes. The bronze and limestone bar defines one edge, under a hammered bronze ceiling whose reflective surface recalls the dimpled surface of the river outside.

A prime design challenge was to provide for readily separating or combining the restaurant's two private dining areas -- and for opening the entire interior for larger events. To accomplish this, the architects flanked the main public dining area with two 15-foot-high, 40-foot-long glass partitions that can slide out of sight on tracks with a robust mechanism normally found in aerospace facilities.

Laminated between the glass surfaces of these partitions — and making them translucent — are commissioned wall-sized artworks by the Dutch artist and graphic designer Karel Martens. Entitled "Clouds," these works — equally viewable from both sides — are composed of innumerable small circular figures, their colors subtly calibrated so that from a distance they read as images of cloud formations. The same kind of laminated panels continue the art installation by Martens in the translucent partitions between the restaurant and the building lobby.

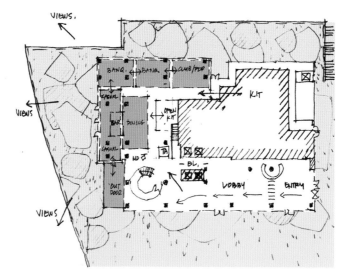

1 Entry
2 Greeter
3 Beverage/Service
4 Waiting
5 Dining Platform
6 Bar
7 Dining
8 Outdoor Dining
9 Small Private Dining Room
10 Large Private Dining Room
11 Sliding Partition
12 Sliding Art Wall
C Coats
KIT Kitchen

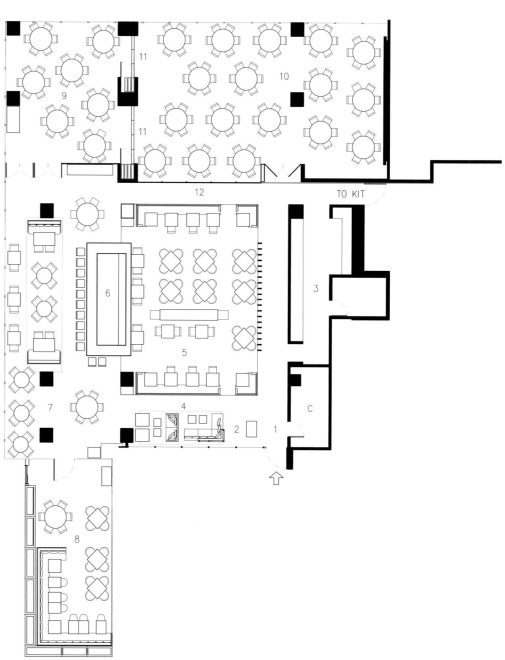

6,300 sq ft/300 seats

Tables along river-facing wall, under rippling hammered bronze ceiling

Dining platform under bronze trellis dotted with lights

Beyond dining platform, private dining room that can be closed off by translucent movable partition (above and below)

One of several translucent partitions seen close-up (facing page), revealing small medallions that form cloud patterns

Over bar, metal canopy above lower hammered bronze trellis

Informal outdoor dining area along riverfront

Island Creek Oyster Bar

Boston, Massachusetts

The design inspiration for this restaurant drew directly on the eponymous source of its shellfish: the creek flowing into Duxbury Bay where Island Creek Oysters are lovingly nurtured. The muted colors and textures of those Massachusetts coastal waters envelop guests as soon as they step in from bustling Kenmore Square, with its busy subway station, close to both Boston University and the Fenway Park baseball mecca.

In the relatively tranquil interior, reclaimed snow fence planks have been repurposed to create adjustable shutters that filter daylight and views throughout the day and evening. Jet Mist granite bar and counter surfaces recall the shades of gray inside and outside oyster shells. Reclaimed white oak flooring and wainscot evoke the timber ribs of old oyster sloops. Banquettes are framed in bleached white oak, and their pale gray polyester-nylon upholstery is tufted in a pattern like that of the seats on oyster farmers' workaday motorboats.

Lighting and ceiling treatment maintain the subtle reference to the Duxbury Bay environment. Much of the ceiling is covered in bands of Tectum painted dull silver. In the bar area, suspended cages of expanded wire mesh — like those that young oysters are grown in — contain acoustical batts. At the transition between the front and rear dining areas hangs a "chandelier" composed of 35 industrial downlights, similar to those in Oyster Creek's Duxbury wharf structures, contained in stainless steel cages that pick up glints from the fixtures inside them.

The centerpiece of the restaurant's plan is the shucking station, with its highlighted display of oysters. It occupies a pivotal position along the length of the bar, which continues into the rear dining room, thus reducing the expectation of a more formal atmosphere there. In fact, many patrons choose to dine at the bar — in venerable oyster bar tradition. The restaurant's kitchens are on the floor above, and restrooms are available off the adjacent lobby of the Hotel Commonwealth.

The ample wall areas in the rear dining room accommodate two distinctive but equally fitting installations. Covering one of these walls is a 38-foot-long photograph by Stephen Sheffield showing oyster cages in the bay at low tide — in an unexpectedly inverted image. Cladding the adjoining wall is an assemblage by the architects, displaying tens of thousands of oyster shells in galvanized steel mesh containers, each of its 23 roughly 2-foot-by-4-foot panels weighing some 300 pounds. The shells were collected by restaurateur Garrett Harker from several restaurants — his own and others. All of them were cleaned by hand and run through dishwashers to sanitize them, then stacked horizontally in these cages. The dedication of the restaurant to oysters is quietly but unmistakably confirmed.

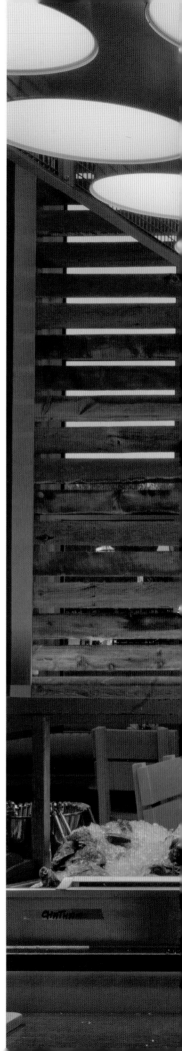

Interior partially shielded from its busy setting by shutters of reclaimed snow fence boards

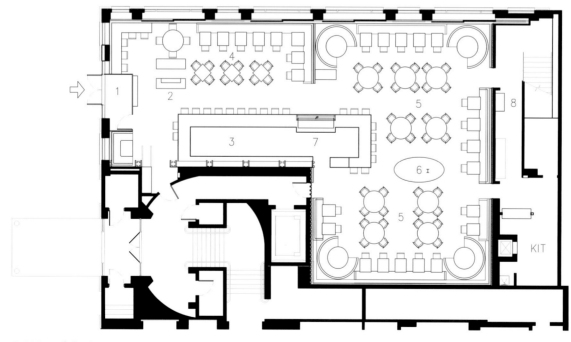

1   Entry
2   Greeter
3   Bar
4   Casual Dining
5   Dining
6   Display Table
7   Shucking Station
8   Beverage Service
KIT Kitchen

5,500 sq ft/150 seats

Bar extending into rear dining room, offering oysters as well as drinks

Bar area with down-lighting bound by baffles of Tectum painted dull silver

Photo of oyster cages at low tide, inverted, covering one wall of dining area

Adjoining wall displaying tens of thousands of oyster shells in galvanized steel mesh containers

Banquettes along dining area wall upholstered in gray fabric

Circular tables with curved banquettes at corners of space

Colicchio & Sons

New York, New York

Originally opened as Craftsteak, chef Tom Colicchio's second New York restaurant shares many characteristics with his first one, Craft. Like the original Craft and subsequent ones in other cities, the architecture here is intended to embody his dedication to straightforward culinary craftsmanship.

Located in the former industrial neighborhood transformed with the opening of the High Line, Colicchio & Sons occupies the 100-year-old shell of a National Biscuit Company bakery building. More expansive than the earlier Craft, this space — 16 feet high and almost 100 feet deep — is clearly divided into an intimate-feeling "tap room" upfront and a dining room beyond, where the feeling of spaciousness is enhanced by extensive windows along the south wall. Including the tap room and the more intimate private dining room, the restaurant has a total seating of 222.

While visible wine storage had been a feature of earlier Craft restaurants, the steel-framed 2,000-bottle wine vault here serves as the divider between the two principal spaces. The spatial compression and release thus created provide varying degrees of intimacy while preserving the communal, refectory quality that Colicchio sought. A steel spiral stair to the upper wine racks occupies a key position at the portal from the tap room to the main dining room.

The restaurant's straightforward materials and details play on the exposed structural systems of the former factory. Existing and new elements complement each other and modulate the scale of the extra-tall volumes. The original riveted steel columns remain exposed, with required fireproofing provided by intumescent paint. Juxtaposed to these industrial components are the steel-and-glass wine vault and a new dining room wall of rough plaster and blackened steel.

A patterned ceiling of oak, bronze, and steel lends intimacy to the tap room, while the dining room extends up to the original concrete vaults, adorned only by the steel plates from which Nabisco's bakery equipment used to hang. Lighting tubes suspended on blackened steel rods enhance the sense of a once-industrial environment. Floors are of blackened oak, with insets in the dining room of custom-designed carpets that echo the colors and irregular linear patterns of the ceiling. An 8' x 12' painting by Stephen Hannock, depicting the High Line in its setting, fills most of the dining room's end wall, acting — as do art works in other restaurants by the firm — to turn a termination into a kind of window.

All furnishings and fittings, such as the cherry wood and steel dining tables, were designed to celebrate their materials and assemblage. The absence of any protective coating on oak, steel, and leather — other than beeswax — promotes their natural ability to age with grace.

Tap room just inside entrance, with massive steel columns and tall wine rack setting design theme

Raw bar, with blackened oak screen and bronze mesh from ceiling forming backdrop

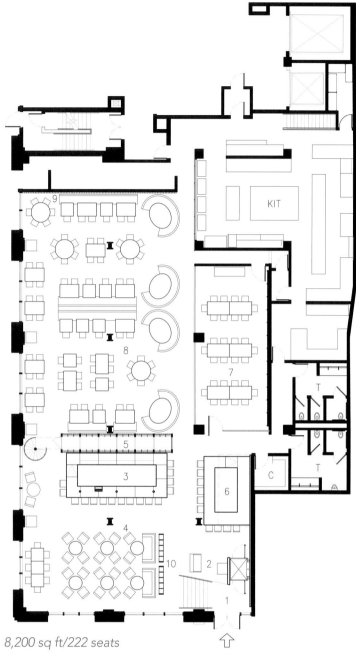

8,200 sq ft/222 seats

1 Entry
2 Greeter
3 Bar
4 Casual Dining
5 Wine Display
6 Raw Bar
7 Private Dining Room
8 Dining
9 Artwork
10 Firewood Display
C Coats
T Toilets
KIT Kitchen

Detail of wine rack and suspended lighting

On walls, bronze mesh, blackened steel and oak

Private dining room with blackened steel end wall, ribbed wall and ceiling of oak and wool

Steel spiral stair to wine rack at passage from tap room to main dining room

New York Central

New York, New York

As part of the renovation of the Grand Hyatt Hotel's vast multilevel lobby, the architects were commissioned to create an essentially new restaurant opening off of it, with a bold identity of its own. A new name, New York Central, alluded both to its pivotal location — between Grand Central Terminal and the Chrysler Building — and to the once powerful railroad company that built the station and initiated the neighborhood's prosperity.

When the 1920s Commodore Hotel was remodeled in 1980 as the Grand Hyatt, the city had permitted a second-floor, glass-enclosed projection over the 42nd Street sidewalk, from which patrons could see literally from river to river across the midsection of Manhattan. While the view out from this space was intriguing, one objective of the restaurant redesign was to attract the attention of the throngs below to this hovering tube — encouraging them to find their way up into it.

The route to the restaurant, through the hotel lobby, had never been obvious, and the redesign eased it in two ways. Post-1980 renovations that had isolated the restaurant from the lobby were removed, restoring the earlier visual continuity. And a new elevator was installed, providing a universally accessible alternative to the elegant but rather roundabout stairs up from both street level and the elevated lobby floor.

A key design challenge was to provide design unity for this long narrow restaurant space, which had to be divided along its length into functional zones — a bar, related casual seating, and more formal dining at tables. The multipurpose solution was a suspended sculpture, some 100 feet long, of polished stainless steel lighting tubes. This architect-designed installation is striking enough to assert the restaurant's identity over its entire length — while also making it prominently visible from the lobby below and from busy 42nd Street.

The bar is internally illuminated through its semi-translucent countertop surfaces, and it faces a continuously glazed wall incorporating video screens — a glowing combination clearly visible to pedestrians passing by. At the opposite end of the restaurant, the more formal dining area adjoins an open kitchen. A more secluded room-like space behind the bar area is devoted to a "wine library" with a communal tasting table. A blue and white composition by the artist Per Fronth adorns the wine rack between this space and the bar.

The interior surfaces of the projection's metal framing are painted dark blue, which the architects find is the best way to minimize its presence in the view out. Ceiling panels of the same dark blue suggest the unlimited depth of the night sky. Louvers under the glazed roof of the projection diffuse sunlight striking it and fill the space with reflected illumination.

Restaurant's greenhouse-like extension projecting over 42ⁿᵈ Street

Lounge area with sculptural assembly of polished stainless steel lighting tubes uniting diverse spaces

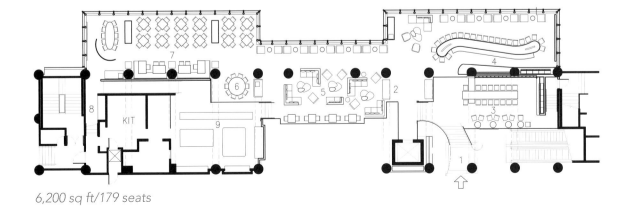

1   Entry
2   Greeter
3   Wine Bar
4   Bar
5   Lounge
6   Chef's Table
7   Dining
8   Beverage/Service
9   Display Kitchen
KIT   Kitchen

6,200 sq ft/179 seats

Bar with internally illuminated semi-translucent top; dining area at far end of space

"Wine library" with tasting table, abstract composition by Per Fronth on translucent wine rack

North End Grill

New York, New York

Located in Battery Park City on the Lower Manhattan waterfront, North End Grill is a re-imagined version of the traditional American bar and grill. The original chef with whom the kitchen was designed used charcoal grilling techniques he learned from both Spain and India to highlight the flavors of the carefully sourced seasonal ingredients, with a stress on seafood. The design takes its cue from this simple and direct method of cooking. To emphasize the process of preparing the food, the plan ensures that all guests have a view into the open kitchen to see cooking taking place at the custom-designed grills.

The almost 175-feet-long street frontage of the restaurant's 8,500-square-foot space is interrupted by a pair of utility rooms for the base building, which effectively divide its length into two distinct parts. Moreover, the space has very little depth, so that back-of-house food-related functions that would typically be tucked far from the guests' view had to be situated in areas that diners would also need to occupy or walk through.

These space limitations provided the impetus for a plan that enhances the guest's experience, rather than detracting from it. In the design, the long journey from the initial greeting at the door to one's seat in the dining room is enlivened by the opportunities en route to see, hear, and smell the grilling of food in the open kitchen from a dining counter directly adjoining it, to walk between the activities at the seafood and pastry stations, and to select a bottle from the glass-fronted wine room before arriving at one's table. While the design maximizes views from the dining room towards the nearby Hudson River, it also allows diners to enjoy views back towards the lively kitchen and food preparation areas through which they have passed.

The material palette — cleft black slate, honed white marble, ebonized white oak, weathered gray pine, and waxed blackened steel — refers to the simplicity of the method of cooking in general and to the charcoal and the food that is grilled over it in particular. For instance, to reinforce the relationship between the architecture and the method by which the chef cooks, the rear wall of the dining room is made of charred poplar planks that are raked with light to accentuate their texture and color.

Outdoor dining area, looking in toward bar

1 Entry
2 Greeter
3 Casual Dining
4 Bar
5 Display Kitchen Dining
6 Pastry/Dessert/ Coffee
7 Fish Prep Area
8 Refrigerated Display
9 Wine Display
10 Service
11 Dining
12 Display Kitchen
13 Private Dining Room
14 Reservations
15 Outdoor Dining
C Coats
T Toilets
KIT Kitchen

8,500 sq ft/181 seats

Bar area, open kitchen visible at left, greeter station at right

Counter dining facing into open kitchen

Flooring pattern marking passage toward dining room

Path to dining room passing between seafood and dessert stations

Contrast of dark furnishings with white linens echoed in high-contrast artworks and patterns of ceilings and lighting

Club 432

New York, New York

As the world's tallest residential tower was about to rise at 432 Park Avenue, Bentel & Bentel were commissioned to design a suite of resident amenities on the structure's sixth floor. The project encompasses 7,000 square feet of interior space and 5,000 square feet of roof terrace. Developer Harry Macklowe invited the architects to help draft the program for this space and to design the interiors and terrace. The two major divisions of the interior are intended to meet the daily needs of residents — the dining room offering regular food service and the lounge accommodating such activities as cocktail and tea service, music, or simply socializing. For special occasions, both interiors plus the terrace are to be combined as one coordinated venue.

The noble proportions of the two principal volumes here — 22.5 feet by 80 feet in floor area, 25 feet high, with 10-foot-square areas of glass framed by massive concrete structural members — presented Bentel & Bentel with unusual opportunities and challenges. These impressive dimensions could seem overwhelming for activities that often call for a feeling of intimacy.

Among the elements that deal with this spatial challenge, the most prominent are the chandeliers. They are not the conventional decorative sources of light, but objects of a scale and volume that become part of the architecture, as essential to the experience of the space as the walls and the floors. In both main rooms, these suspended creations allow residents to understand their relationship to the rooms along both their long axes and in the dimensions between floor and ceiling.

In the lounge, two very tall chandeliers with the sparkle of lead crystal hang down to a level in proportion to human occupants, and they imply the existence of two volumes of more comfortable scale. On the dining side, the suspended lighting forms a horizontal plane to keep the extra-tall space from just trailing off into darkness. It is also a conscious homage to the Richard Lippold sculpture over the bar at the landmark Four Seasons Restaurant nearby.

The club design also acknowledges its unique setting within the tower shaped by Rafael Viñoly Architects. Bentel & Bentel strove to exhibit a geometrical discipline and restrained color palette characteristic of the structure as a whole. To this end, they have employed a variety of contrasting but complementary materials — reflective black and white marble on the lobby floor, subtly echoed in earth-toned carpet elsewhere, sparkling crystal in some chandeliers, softly glowing glass in others, walls of suede in the dining room, white oak in the lounge, ceilings clad with mirrored metal and oak panels — each material exhibiting its own color, finish, and cadence of joints.

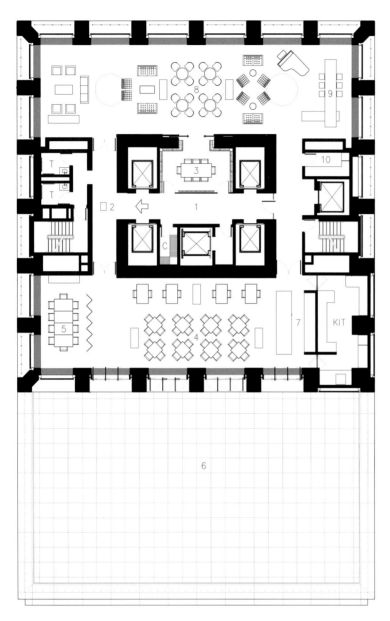

7,000 sq ft/101 seats

1   Entry
2   Greeter
3   Wine Room
4   Dining
5   Private Dining Room
6   Outdoor Terrace
7   Display Kitchen
8   Lounge
9   Bar
10 Beverage/Service
C   Coats
T   Toilets
KIT Kitchen

Entry via elevator lobby with black and white marble floor, walls of polished steel and translucent glass

Section of lounge, showing white oak walls, oak and mirrored metal ceiling, tall chandeliers

Elevation drawing of lounge, with crystal chandeliers and fabric drapery

Crystal chandelier, mirrored metal ceiling

Lounge, with carpet subtly echoing lobby floor, multipurpose bar at far end

Lounge wall of herringbone patterned white oak

Wine rack behind translucent patterned glass

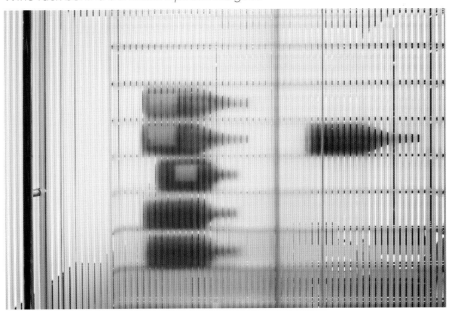

In dining room, suede walls, tubular glass chandelier, suspended globes

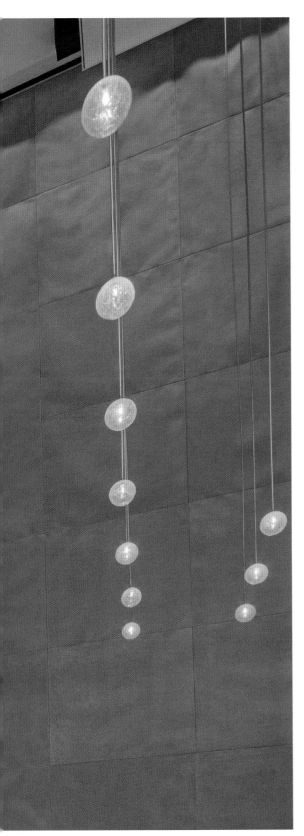

Canopy of suspended globe lighting over dining room

Dining area with open kitchen

OTHER BENTEL & BENTEL RESTAURANTS: A Selection

ALIANTE MARKET | Las Vegas, NV
Arch Photo, Inc.

AMERICAN CRAFT | Chicago, IL
James Steinkamp Photography

ASHTON CIGAR BAR | Philadelphia, PA
Arch Photo, Inc.

B&G OYSTER | Boston, MA
Arch Photo, Inc.

BIG BAR AT HYATT REGENCY | Chicago, IL
James Steinkamp Photography

BLUE SMOKE BATTERY PARK CITY | New York, NY

Arch Photo, Inc.

CAFÉ AT THE WHITNEY MUSEUM | New York, NY
with RPBW + Cooper Robertson   *Arch Photo, Inc.*

CASINO BAR | Las Vegas, NV

Bentel and Bentel in collaboration with 3Di

CLARENDON | New York, NY

Bentel and Bentel

CRAFT DALLAS | Dallas, TX

Arch Photo, Inc.

CRAFTSTEAK | Las Vegas, NV

Arch Photo, Inc.

DESCENT BAR AT THE W HOTEL | Boston, MA

Peter Vanderwarker

ELEMENT 47, THE LITTLE NELL | Aspen, CO

Arch Photo, Inc.

GALLERIES AT LEX AT GRAND HYATT | New York, NY

Arch Photo, Inc.

HEARTH | New York, NY

Arch Photo, Inc.

HERITAGE STEAK AT THE MIRAGE HOTEL |
Las Vegas, NV   *Arch Photo, Inc.*

HUDSON GARDEN GRILL AT THE NEW YORK
BOTANICAL GARDEN | Bronx, NY   *Arch Photo, Inc.*

HYATT REGENCY CHICAGO | Chicago, IL

James Steinkamp Photography

INSIEME | New York, NY

Arch Photo, Inc.

JOSE ANDRES RESTAURANT | Las Vegas, NV

Bentel and Bentel

KIAWAH ISLAND RIVER CLUB | Johns Island, SC

Arch Photo, Inc.

MARKET AT THE HYATT REGENCY | Chicago, IL

James Steinkamp Photography

MᶜCRADY'S TAVERN | Charleston, SC

Andrew Celbuka Photography

MEDÍ | New York, NY
Arch Photo, Inc.

PLANE FOOD BY GORDON RAMSAY |
Heathrow Airport, England

PRIVÉ | New York, NY
Arch Photo, Inc.

ROUGE TOMATE CHELSEA | New York, NY
Bentel and Bentel

ROW 34 | Boston, MA
Arch Photo, Inc.

STETSON'S GRILL | Chicago, IL
James Steinkamp Photography

THE BUTCHER SHOP | Boston, MA

Peter Vanderwarker

UNION LEAGUE CLUB | New York, NY

Arch Photo, Inc.

UNTITLED | New York, NY
with RPBW + Cooper & Robertson   *Arch Photo, Inc.*

'WICHCRAFT | Las Vegas, NV

Arch Photo, Inc.

'WICHCRAFT | San Francisco, CA
with Mark Horton   *Arch Photo, Inc.*

ZYLO | Hoboken, NJ

Arch Photo, Inc.

Artworks

Artworks in Bentel & Bentel restaurants are not just ornaments — or trophies. They contribute to the spatial experience, serving as focal points or as perceptual openings in the walls that often confine restaurants. Many of them are commissioned, some are lucky finds. Works subject to contact with people are encased in glass, readily reproducible, or both.

The Modern, *Clearing*, Thomas Demand

Aldo Sohm Wine Bar, *Untitled*, Cat Man

Gramercy Tavern, *Cornucopia*, Robert Kushner

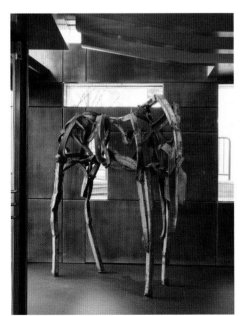

Houston's, *Untitled*, Deborah Butterfield

The Modern, *Broken Bands of Color in Four Directions*, Sol LeWitt

Aldo Sohm Wine Bar, *Wall Drawing*, Sol LeWitt

Le Bernardin, *Deep Water,* Ran Ortner

Riverpark, *Dutch Clouds,* Karel Martens

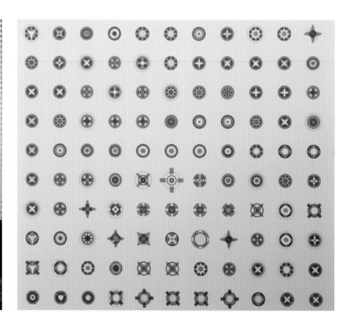

Cielo, *Split Sky/Approaching Storm*, Per Fronth

Cielo, *Floating*, Bentel & Bentel

Element 47, Little Nell, *Untitled*,
Michelle Grabner

Ground Café, Yale University, digital art

Island Creek Oyster Bar, *Island Creek*, Stephen Sheffield

Craft, *Squid Boats on the Gulf of Siam*,
Stephen Hannock

Colicchio & Sons, *River Light*, Robert Hammond

Eleven Madison Park, *Madison Square Park at the Turn of the Century*, Stephen Hannock

Craftsteak Las Vegas, *To Be Alive Is Pure Luck*, Per Fronth

Craft Atlanta, *Animal Series, Filet*, Stephanie Jordan

Grand Hyatt Galleries on Lex, New York, *The Walking Horizon IV,* Burghard Müller-Dannhausen

Rouge Tomate, *Photosynthesis,* Per Fronth

Stetson's Private Dining Room at Hyatt Regency, Chicago, *Furrowed,* Ben Butler

Market at Hyatt Regency, Chicago, *Containment,* James Kennedy

American Craft at Hyatt Regency, Chicago, *The Lake*, Ben Butler

Bentel & Bentel

Architects · Interior Designers · Staff

Current:
Paul Bentel
Carol Rusche Bentel
Peter Bentel
Susan Nagle
Thomas O'Connor
Raffaele Razzano
Matthew Casamassina
Alison Singer
Ashley Cuoco
Jennifer Glasser
Ann Gerin
Parisa Ooriel
Yvette Canales
Matthew Buchheit
Alexander Chamoun
James Giustiniani

Former:
Sara Abd Rabbo
Peter Alexiadis
Lauren Ascani
Kojo Asiedo
Cherie Baldenko
Dan Beckman
Eric Biamonte
Lara Leigh Brugo
Christine Caine
Peter Campanella
Jesse Cardenas

Michelle Cardillo
Robert Costello
Benedict Cruz
Sylvia Dejoie
DiAnna Dezago
Kristen Emory
Tahmina Gaffar
Nesma Galal
Joseph Gallinaro
Jesse Ganes
Luigi Gileno
Gregory Goldstone
Benjamin Gorelick
Alyssa Grella
Michael Grella
Jocelyn Hain
Peter Halkias
Laura Hanshe
Tiffany Hicks
Chris Hinchey
Kafi Iwuoha
Ken Jerome
Kevin Kawiecki
Michael Kranyak
Melanie Li Foo Wing
Annie Lo
Boone Lo
Thomas Lozada
Adolfo Martinez
Brian McCabe

Kevin Meussig
Abe Medina
Marc Mucciacci
Caroline Neely
Jessica O'Regan
Justin Paraiso
Daniella Parra
Scott Pavick
Carlos Pereira
Nisha Prasad
Gregory Preus
Misa Radulov
Jeff Reid
Pam Rice
Laila Roising
Mike Rubenstein
Rosanna Russo
Patricia Sands
Milan Savanovic
Tom Scavo
Kelley Schultz
Jurg Schupbach
Michael Sheedy
John Soliman
Keith Striza
Gregory Thomas
Nancy Versaci
Matt Wasnewsky
Paul Wise

Consultants

Associate Architects:
Bauer Latoza Studio
Cooper Robertson
Friedmutter Group
HKS Architects
KGA Architecture
Klai Juba Wald Architects
Li Salzman Architects
Mark Horton Architecture
Reggie Gibson Architects
Renzo Piano Building Workshop
SLCE Architects
Spagnolo Gisness & Associates, Inc.
SPG3
TRO Jung|Brannen

Structural Engineers:
Alfred Benesch & Company
Koutsoubis, Alonso Associates PE PC
McNamara - Salvia
Robert Silman Associates
Shmerykowsky Consulting Engineers

MEPS Engineers:
Altieri Sebor Wieber LLC
AMA Consulting Engineers
BLW Engineers
Driscoll Electric
Grumman/Butkus Associates
WSP Parsons Brinkerhoff

Lighting Consultants:
Focus Lighting
Hillman DiBernardo Leiter Castelli Lighting Design
Horton Lees Brogden Lighting Design
Kaplan Gehring McCarroll Architectural Lighting
L'Observatoire International

Food Service Consultants:
Alliance Food Equipment
Clevenger Frable LaVallee Consulting and Design
Jacobs Doland Beer
James Davella Studio
KDS Consulting and Design
Next Step Design

Romano Gatland Food Service Consultants
TriMark Food Service Equipment Supplies and Design

Photographers:
Andrew Celbuka Photography
Arch Photo Inc.
Gustav Hoiland, Photographer
James Steinkamp, Photographer
Oleg March, Photographer
Peter Vanderwarker, Photographer

Contractors:
The Allied Group
Cafco Construction Management
CDS Mestel Construction
E W Howell
Guerdon Modular Buildings
Jadum Construction
James McHugh Construction Co.
MG & Company
Shawmut Design and Construction
Structure Tone LLC

Millworkers/Metalworkers:
A.G. Mastercraft
Architectural Woodwork Industries, Inc.
Bauerschmidt and Sons
Flowerbox
Hudec Woodworking Corp.
Lasvit
Levolux
Lukas Lighting
M. Cohen & Sons
Mark Richey Woodworking
Recycled Brooklyn
Unique Statements in Wood
Veyko
Workspace 11

Specialty Furniture Manufacturers:
Brueton
Dine Rite Seating
Jay's Furniture Products
Mark Albrecht Studio

Awards

2017

Excellence in Historic Preservation Awards, Preservation League of New York State, Rouge Tomate Chelsea, New York, NY

International Design Awards, Silver, Rouge Tomate Chelsea, New York, NY

NYCxDesign Awards, Finalist, Rouge Tomate Chelsea, New York, NY

NYCxDesign Awards, Finalist, Club 432, New York, NY

2016

SARA National Awards, Interior Design Award, Riverpark, New York, NY

SARA NY Design Awards, Interior Design Award, Riverpark, New York, NY

James Beard Award, Untitled at The Whitney (With Renzo Piano Building Workshop and Cooper Robertson)

CODAWORX, CODAawards, American Craft Restaurant, Hyatt Regency Chicago

Interior Design Magazine BOY Awards, Hospitality Finalist, Club 432, New York, NY

ARCHI Awards: AIA Long Island Chapter, Benjamin Moore & Co. Color Award, Rouge Tomate Chelsea, New York, NY

ARCHI Awards: AIA Long Island Chapter, Enterprise Lighting Sales Lighting Award, Club 432, New York, NY

2015

SARA National Awards, Design Award of Honor, Ground Café at Yale, New Haven, CT

SARA National Awards, Design Award of Honor, Aldo Sohm Wine Bar, New York, NY

ARCHI Awards: AIA Long Island Chapter, Commendation for Hospitality, Heritage Steak at Mirage, Las Vegas, NV

2014

International Design Awards, Interior Designer of the Year – Silver, Ground Café at Yale, New Haven, CT

SARA National Awards, Design Award of Merit, Ashton Cigar Bar, Philadelphia, PA

SARA National Awards, Design Award of Honor, Hyatt Regency Chicago, IL

Hospitality Design Magazine Awards, Hyatt Regency Chicago, Chicago, IL

A' Design Award, Silver - Winner for Interior Space and Exhibition Design Category, Ground Café at Yale, New Haven, CT

SARA NY Design Awards, Bronze Award of Honor, Island Creek Oyster Bar, Boston, MA

SARA NY Design Awards, Silver Award of Merit, Heritage Steak at The Mirage, Las Vegas, NV

AIA Small Project Awards, Ground Café at Yale, New Haven, CT

ASID NY Metro Chapter, Designer of Distinction Award

ARCHI Awards: AIA Long Island Chapter, Interior Architecture Award, Riverpark, New York, NY

ARCHI Awards: AIA Long Island Chapter, Small Project Award, Ground Café at Yale, New Haven, CT

ARCHI Awards: AIA Long Island Chapter, Hospitality Award, Hyatt Regency Chicago, IL

2013

Contract Magazine Awards, Best Hotel Interior, Grand Hyatt New York, NY

SARA NY Design Awards, Award of Merit, Grand Hyatt New York, NY

SARA NY Design Awards, Award of Merit, Riverpark, New York, NY

SARA NY Design Awards, Award of Merit, Le Bernardin, New York, NY

2012

SARA National Awards, Design Award of Honor, Grand Hyatt New York, NY
SARA National Awards, Design Award of Honor for Light Fixture, Grand Hyatt New York, NY
SARA National Awards, Design Award of Merit, Le Bernardin, New York, NY
James Beard Award, Best Restaurant, Le Bernardin, New York, NY
BDNY Gold Key Awards, Fine Dining, Le Bernardin, New York, NY
SARA Scope Awards, Design Award of Merit, Le Bernardin, New York, NY
Interior Design Magazine BOY Awards, Hospitality/Fine Dining, Le Bernardin, New York, NY
AIA New York State Design Awards, Citation, Riverpark, New York, NY

2011

SARA National Awards, Market at Grand Hyatt New York, NY
AIA New York State Awards, Award of Excellence, Toku, Manhasset, NY
SARA NY Design Awards, Design Award of Honor, Craft Atlanta, GA
SARA NY Design Awards, Design Award of Honor, Rouge Tomate, New York, NY
ARCHI Awards: AIA Long Island Chapter, Best Interior, Apella at Alexandria Center, New York, NY

2010

SARA National Awards, Design Award of Recognition, Toku, Manhasset, NY
SARA National Awards, Design Award of Honor, Craft Atlanta, GA
SARA National Awards, Design Award of Merit, W Boston Hotel, MA
Contract Magazine Inspirations Awards, Honorable Mention, Rouge Tomate, New York, NY
Boston Society of Architects, Award for Design, W Boston Hotel, MA
AIA New York State Design Awards, Citation for Design, Rouge Tomate, New York, NY
AIA New York State Design Awards, Excellence in Interior Architecture, Colicchio & Sons, New York, NY
ARCHI Awards: AIA Long Island Chapter, Hospitality Award, W Hotel Boston, MA
AIA Honors Awards, Craftsteak, New York, NY

2009

SARA National Awards, Design Award of Honor, Rouge Tomate, New York, NY
SARA NY Design Awards, Design Award of Honor, Toku, Manhasset, NY
Contract Magazine Awards, Honorable Mention, Rouge Tomate, New York, NY
ARCHI Awards: AIA Long Island Chapter, Lighting Award, Zylo at the W Hotel Hoboken, NJ
ARCHI Awards: AIA Long Island Chapter, Hospitality Award, Rouge Tomate, New York, NY

2008

Contract Magazine, Interiors Award, Craftsteak, New York, NY
AIA New York State Design Awards, Toku, Manhasset, NY
AIA New York City Chapter Awards, Interior Award of Excellence, Craftsteak, New York, NY
ARCHI Awards: AIA Long Island Chapter, Design Award, Toku, Manhasset, NY

2007

SARA National Design Awards, Craftsteak, New York, NY
SARA NY Design Awards, Café 2 at MoMA, New York, NY
AIA New York State Design Awards, Craftsteak, New York, NY
AIA New York State Design Awards, Best Interior Design, The Modern at MoMA, New York, NY

Hospitality Design Magazine, Platinum Circle Award, Bentel & Bentel Architects/Planners
AIA Los Angeles Chapter Awards, Best Interior Award Finalist, Craft Los Angeles, CA
Glass Association of North America, Glass Awards, Cielo, Boca Raton, FL
Contract Magazine Awards, Craftsteak, New York, NY
Contract Magazine Awards, The Modern at MoMA, New York, NY
ARCHI Awards: AIA Long Island Chapter, Interior Architecture, Craftsteak Las Vegas

2006

Wallpaper Magazine International Awards, Best Restaurant Design, The Modern at MOMA, New York, NY
SARA National Design Awards, Design Award of Merit, Café 2 at MoMA, New York, NY
SARA National Design Awards, Design Award of Merit, The Modern at MoMA, New York, NY
Contract Magazine National Awards, Best Restaurant Design, The Modern at MoMA, New York, NY
James Beard Awards, Best Restaurant Design, The Modern at MoMA, New York, NY
ARCHI Awards: AIA Long Island Chapter, Interior Architecture, Café 2 at MoMA, New York, NY

2005

Interior Design Magazine with IIDA, Best New Restaurant, The Modern at MoMA, New York, NY
Esquire Magazine, Best New Restaurant, The Modern at MoMA, New York, NY
Contract Magazine, Interiors Award, The Modern at MoMA, New York, NY
BDNY Gold Key Award, Hospitality, The Modern at MoMA, New York, NY
AIA New York City Chapter, Best Interior, The Modern at MoMA, New York, NY
ARCHI Awards: AIA Long Island Chapter, Excellence in Architecture, The Modern at MoMA, New York, NY

2004

ARCHI Awards: AIA Long Island Chapter, Design Award, Houston's Restaurant, Boston, MA
ARCHI Awards: AIA Long Island Chapter, Design Award, The Modern at MoMA, New York, NY

2003

SARA National Design Awards, Houston's Restaurant, Boston, MA
ARCHI Awards: AIA Long Island Chapter, Gold Archi Award, Craft, New York, NY

2002

AIA New York State Design Awards, Award of Merit, Craft, New York, NY

2001

Time Out New York, Best Restaurant Design of the Year, Craft, New York, NY

2000

Interior Design Magazine with IIDA, Best Design of the Year, Eleven Madison Park, New York, NY
ARCHI Awards: AIA Long Island Chapter, Design Award, Eleven Madison Park, New York, NY

1996

ARCHI Awards: AIA Long Island Chapter, Design Award, Gramercy Tavern, New York, NY

Publications

Aldo Sohm Wine Bar

Block, Annie. "Bentel & Bentel designs Aldo Sohm Wine Bar in New York." *Interior Design*, February 23, 2015.

Cooper, Zoe. "Why Not Unwind at One of These 7 Wine Bars." *Architizer,* July 27, 2015.

Leland, J. "It's Casual at Le Bernardin's Baby Brother." *The New York Times*, October 25, 2014.

"Looking Ahead." *The New York Times,* April 24, 2013: D6.

Le Bernardin

Akkam, Alia. "Dressing Down." *Hospitality Design*, March, 2012: 47-48.

Block, Annie. "A Sea Change: Paul and Carol Bentel reinvent New York's Le Bernardin for Eric Ripert." *Interior Design,* January, 2012: 41-44.

Green, Gael. "Sorry, Bentel & Bentel are the architects of Le Bernardin's big makeover." *Insatiable Critic,* September 5, 2011.

Herrera, Tim. "NYC'S Top Eats." *Newsday*, October 3, 2012, sec. NYC: A36-A37.

Wells, Pete. "Moving Ever Forward, Like A Fish." *The New York Times*, May 23, 2012: D1, D6.

"Eric Ripert, New York's Seafood Master." *Wine Spectator,* August, 2014: cover.

"Nouvelle Ripert." *New York*, December 19, 2011: 90.

"Off the Menu: Looking Ahead: Le Bernardin Privé and Aldo Sohm Wine Bar." *The New York Times,* April 24, 2013: D6.

B&G Oysters

Hall, Alexandra. "The Heat is On." *Boston Magazine's Concierge*, Spring 2004: 59-60.

Blue Smoke

"American." *Time Out New York: Eating and Drinking*, 2002: 15.

Café 2 at MoMA

"Archi Awards Honor Excellence." *House*, January-February, 2007: 152.

"Dansk Invasion: New York, MOMA." *Bo Bedre*, No. 1, 2005: 102-105.

"MoMA Returns." *Contract,* December, 2004: 12.

Cielo

"2008 Crystal Achievement & Awards: Most Innovative Interior Glass Application." *Glass Magazine*, October, 2008: 42.

Club 432

Fabricant, Florence. "Shaun Hergatt's Next Restaurant: Elevated and Exclusive." *The New York Times*, July 18, 2016.

Macklowe, Harry, ed. *432*, New York: CIM Group, 2015: 190-191, 195, 198, 202.

"Best of Year Honorees." *Interior Design*, December, 2016: 108.

Colicchio & Sons

Alati, Danine. "Interior Awards: Restaurant." *Contract,* January, 2008: 88-91.

Robertson, Tim. "Top-Ranked Designs merge Old and New." *Newsday,* December 24, 2007: D1-D3.

Sternbergh, Adam. "The Highline." *New York,* May 7, 2007: 26-31.

Craft Dallas

Dillon, David. "W Dallas Victory Hotel & Residences." *Architectural Record,* October 2007: 146-147.

Craft

AIA 2010-2012: Designs for the New Decade, Hong Kong: Design Media, 201.

Gold, Jonathan. "Diners Can Be Choosers." *Gourmet,* August, 2001: 48, 117.

Grimes, William. "Restaurants." *The New York Times,* June 27, 2001: F7.

Novick, Susan Morris. "Craftsmanship." *Elements,* Spring 1995: 116-120.

Platt, Adam. "Arts And Craft." *New York,* May, 2001: 65-66.

"A modern-day tandem recalling Greene and Greene, Bentel & Bentel imbue Craft with remarkable details."
   Architectural Record, November, 2002: 244-248.

"Honor Award Interiors." *Architectural Record,* May, 2003: 159.

"Honor Award in Interiors." *Architectural Record,* February, 2003: 52.

"The NEW New York." *Casa,* October, 2007: 76.

Craftsteak Las Vegas

Lindberg, Peter Jon. "Raising the Stakes." *Travel + Leisure,* December, 2002: 163-167, 199-201.

"Hot Tables." *Conde Nast Traveler,* May, 2004: 137-146.

Craft Los Angeles

Nunn, Jennie. "Space Craft." *California Home + Design,* 2008: 128-129.

"Play Honor Award." *The Registry,* April, 2010: 20.

Eleven Madison Park

Berman, Holly. "Building a Buzz." *Food Arts,* September, 1998: 166.

Geran, Monica. "IIDA Awards, Best of Competition: Remembering Things Past." *Interior Design,* November, 2000:
   110-113.

Madigan, MJ. "Fraternal Twins." *Restaurants and Institutions,* July 1, 1999: 75-82.

Matthews, Thomas. "World Class." *Wine Spectator,* April 30, 2001: cover, 62-70.

Strand, Oliver. "At Eleven Madison Park, 'Awesome' Beats Acclaim." *The New York Times,* November 8, 2010: D1, D5.

"Dedication by Design." *Food Arts,* May, 1999: 93-96, 98 -100.

Gramercy Tavern

Anthony, Michael, and Dorothy Kalins. *The Gramercy Tavern Cookbook.* New York: Clarkson Potter, 2013.

Bellamy, Gail. *Design Spirits: Bars, Brewpubs & Techno Clubs.* Glen Cove, NY: Interior Details, PBC International: 1995.

Ehrlich, Richard. "What's New." *Weekend,* June 30, 2001: 101.

Kaminsky, Peter. "The Next Great Restaurant." *New York,* July, 1994: cover, 1-8-25.

Radulski, John P. "Gramercy Tavern." *Hospitality Design,* May-June, 1995: 24-28.

Reichl, Ruth. "Restaurants." *The New York Times,* October 14, 1994: C26.

Richmond, Holly. "Warming Trend." *Contract Design,* December, 1995: 32-36.

Stranger, Ila. "Reworking the Room." *Departures,* November-December, 195: 149-154.

"Gramercy Tavern." *Hospitality Design,* September, 1994: 14-15.

Ground Café, Yale University

Manack, Marc and Linda Reeder. *Out of Scale: Small Project Scale Awards.* ORO Editions, 2015: 132-133.

"Caffeine and Creativity." *Yale Engineering Magazine,* 2012: 22-23.

"LED'ing the Way." *Yale Engineering Magazine,* 2013-2014: cover, 29-35.

"Ground Café at Yale University." *A Design Award & Competition, Winning Designs 2013-2014,* Designer Press, 2014: 177.

Hyatt Regency Chicago

"Bentel & Bentel redesigns Hyatt Regency Chicago." *Hotel Design,* April 2, 2013.

Hotel Pulitzer (& restaurant)

"Pulitzer Prize." *Hospitality Design,* April, 2009: 36.

Market Restaurant by Jean-Georges at the W Hotel

Cohen, Edie. "W: Where, When, and Why." *Interior Design,* November, 2009: 89-111.

Fabricant, Florence. "A Master Chef with a New Role." *The New York Times,* August 1, 2001: F3.

First, Devra. "In the Market for Jean-Georges." *Boston Globe,* December 23, 2009: 21-22.

Garlough, Donna. "Where to eat now 2010." *Boston,* January, 2010: 54-56.

Grimes, William. "Restaurants." *The New York Times,* September 19, 2001: F8.

O'Connor, John T. "Through The Looking Glass: W Boston Hotel and Residences." *Esplanade Magazine,* January 1, 2010: 29-30.

Tandy, Catherine. "Q&A with Paul Bentel." *Boutique Design,* January-February, 2010.

"2010 Archi Award Winners." *House,* January- February, 2011: 109.

"Boston welcomes W Hotel." *Hospitality Design,* November, 2009.

"Design Elements." *Lodging Hospitality,* January, 2010: 40.

"Gold Key Finalists." *Interior Design,* October, 2010: 126.

"W Boston: Bentel & Bentel Architects/Planners." *Hammer Magazine,* January 1, 2011: 13.

Medí

Kaminsky, Peter. "Tables for Two." *New York,* August, 2001: 81.

Spilman, Bill. "Specialty Ceilings." *CISCA Interior Construction,* May-June, 2002: cover, 4.

"Correction." *New York,* August-September, 2001: 28.

New York Central at Grand Hyatt NY

Hooper, Emily. "Bentel & Bentel Architects/Planners." *Contract,* January-February, 2013: 74-78.

Serlen, Bruce. "Massive Makeover positions Grand Hyatt NY for Future Success." *Hotel Business Design,* January-February, 2012: 12-14.

"HD Awards Hyatt Regency Chicago." *Hospitality Design,* June, 2014: 153.

"New York Central." *Spirit: Southwest Airlines,* November, 2011: 60.

North End Grill

Wells, Pete. "Veteran Crew sets Imaginative Course." *The New York Times,* March 21, 2012, Sec. Restaurants: D6.

Wilsey, Sean. "Danny Meyer on a Roll." *The New York Times Magazine,* August 7, 2011: 22-27.

"On the Waterfront." *Hospitality Design,* April, 2012: 270-273.

Plane Food

Weeks, Katie. "First Class Dining." *Contract,* June, 2009: 68-72.

"Countdown to Plane Food." *Gordon Ramsay,* March, 2008: 1.

"Plane Food: Gordon Ramsay at Heathrow T5." *Dialogue,* July, 2008: 26-33.

Riverpark

Sifton, Sam. "Intrigue by the East River." *The New York Times,* December 7, 2010.

Zimmern, Andrew. "Food Fight." *SKY DELTA,* June 2016: 48-49.

Rouge Tomate

Adams, Michael. "Ripe and Ready." *Hospitality Design,* August, 2009: 104-105.

Bruni Frank. "Off the Avenue, Virtue Gets a Sexy Dress." *The New York Times,* January 1, 2009.

Cuozzo, Steve. "Bad timing, good dining." *New York Post,* January 28, 2009.

Fronth, Per, and Cecilie Tyri Holt. *Per Fronth.* Oslo: Press Publishing, 2009.

Gordinier, Jeff. "Hold the Butter." *The New York Times,* January 7, 2013.

LaBarre, Suzanne. "Unsung Heroes." *Metropolis,* April, 2009: 80-87.

Latief, Ade. "AHEC 2011 Architectural and Press Mission." *Griya Asri,* December, 2011: 102-104.

Matthew, Kirsten. "You Say Tomato." *Page Six Magazine,* November 16, 2009.

Rago, Danielle, "Open Restaurant." *The Architects Newspaper,* November 19, 2008: 7.

Shindler, Merril. "Favorite Gear." *Food Arts,* January-February, 2013: 44-45, 57.

"Best of 2009 Awards: Rouge Tomate Restaurant." *New York Construction,* December, 2009: 84.

"Eats 'N' Sleeps." *Array: Inside the New York Design Center,* February-March, 2009: 32.

"Inspirations." *Contract,* April, 2009: 22.

"Manhattan's Newest (Red) Hot Spot." *Vanity Fair,* October 2009: 65.

"Rouge Tomate." *House,* January-February, 2010: 105.

"Drink Local." *Sky Delta,* January, 2013: 43.

"What's Hot! News." *Elle: Décor: The Travel Issue,* April, 2009: 46.

Rouge Tomate Chelsea

Asimov, Eric. "Rouge Tomate: Smaller Restaurant, Bigger Wine List." *The New York Times,* September 6, 2016.

Bull, Marian. "Year in Review: The Best Restaurants of 2016." *Departures,* December, 2016: 3.

Diez, Patty. "Rouge Tomate 2.0 Opens Tonight in Chelsea." *Eater New York,* September, 2016.

Gorst, Jake. *Rebuilding Rouge Tomate: Sustainable Design for Sustainable Dining.* Film, 2017.

Landman, Beth. "Michelin-Starred Health-Conscious Restaurant Rouge Tomate to Reopen in the Flatiron." *Eater New York,* October 2014.

Siegel, Emily. "First Look: Rouge Tomate reopens in Chelsea." *Zagat,* September 2016.

"An Autumn Harvest of New Restaurants." *New York Times,* September 9, 2015.

The Modern at MoMA

Alati, Danine. "Large Restaurant." *Contract,* January, 2006: 92-94.

Bruni, Frank. "Inside an Empire, The Power Shifts." *The New York Times,* January 10, 2007: F1, F12.

Cespedes, Analya. "Lenguaje Moderno." *Vivienda Decoracion,* May 14, 2005: 68.

Collin, Glenn. "A Destination for Food (And Some Art, Too)." *The New York Times,* October 27, 2004: F1-F2.

Dixon, John Morris. "Monumental MoMA." *Architecture,* February, 2005: 40-49.

Elder, Sean. "Modern Holiday." *Food & Wine,* December, 2004: 200-209.

Filler, Martin. "BIG MoMA." *House & Garden,* December, 2004: 78-81, 143.

Fussell, Betty. "Food Meets Art." *Food Arts,* January-February, 2005: 46-50.

Lange, Alexandra. "This New House." *New York,* October 18, 2004: 28-30.

Lange, Alexandra. "Modern Meditation." *Metropolis,* June, 2005: 182-188.

Levere, Jane. "Danish Delight." *Hospitality Design,* September-October, 2005: 172-175.

Lowry, Glenn D. *Designing the New Museum of Modern Art.* New York: Museum of Modern Art, 2004.

Nochlin, Linda. "The New Modern: Itineraries." *Art in America,* March, 2005: 50-59.

Novick, Susan Morris. "East as Eden." *Elements,* Summer 2005: 66-70.

Platt, Adam. "Modern Love." *New York,* April 4, 2005: 58-59.

Platt, Adam. "The Next Jean-Georges." *New York,* June 27, 2005: 26.

Riordan, John. *Restaurants by Design.* New York: Collins Design, 2006.

Rudick, Jennifer Ash. "Modern Art Menu." *Veranda,* January-February, 2009: 138-146.

Ryder, Bethan. *New Restaurant Design.* London: Laurence King, 2007: 136-137.

Shoemaker-Rauen, Stacy. "Food and Beverage." *Hospitality Design,* May-June, 2007: 101.

Slonim, Jeffrey. "What's Modern Now?" *Departures,* September, 2005: 216-219.

Stephens, Suzanne. "The Modern, New York City." *Architectural Record,* September, 2005: 124-131.

Stephens, Suzanne. "Museum of Modern Art, New York." *Architectural Record,* January, 2005: 94-109.

Weiss, Sean. *New York: Architecture & Design.* Kempen, Germany: TeNeues, 2007.

Wigley, Mark, Cynthia Davidson, Yve-Alain Bois, and Benjamin H.D. Buchloh, "The New MoMA." *ARTFORUM,* February, 2005: 130-143.

Viladas, Pilar. "Museum Quality." *The New York Times Style Magazine,* Spring, 2005: 20.

"Best New Restaurant." *Wallpaper,* February, 2006: 114.

"Corrections." *The New York Times,* February 9, 2005.

Danish Design Project at MoMA. Montreal: Transcontinental/Litho Acme, 2006.

"Eating Amid Art." *Hospitality Design,* August, 2004: 44.

"Eats 'N' Sleeps." *Array,* Summer, 2005: 70.

"Honor Awards: Interiors." *Architectural Record,* May, 2007: 142.

"Midtown Lunch." *New York,* March, 2005: 65.

"MoMA Returns." *Contract,* December, 2004: 12.

"Must-See Sessions." *Hospitality Design,* May 15, 2008: 16.

"Restaurant of the Year: The Modern, New York." *Esquire,* November, 2005: 134.

"Strategist." *New York,* January 24, 2005: 47.

"The Design Dozen." *Newsweek,* May 23, 2005: 70-71.

Tabla

"Gold Key Finalists: Fine Dining." *Interior Design,* October 2005: 192.

"Tabla." *Food Arts,* September, 1998: 166.

Toku

Holt, Emily. "Something to Savor." *W: A Supplement to W,* December-January, 2006: 99.

Ladd, Wendy. "Standing the Test of Thyme." *Great Restaurants of Long Island,* Fall 2008: 45, 65, 235.

Rigtod, John. "Award Winning Architectural Entries." *Hammer Magazine,* Fall 2009: 10.

Untitled, Whitney Museum

"Museum Quality." *Hospitality Design,* October, 2015: 150-51.

Other

"Education: Carol Bentel, New York College of Technology." *Hospitality Design,* September 2014: 131.

"HD 2007." *Expo & Conference Journal,* May, 2007: cover, 50.

"Lifetime Achievement." *Hospitality Design,* March, 2007: 23-24.

"Looking Back." *Hospitality Design,* July, 2013: 103.

"Platinum Circle." *Hospitality Design,* April, 2007: 164-165.

"Platinum Circle." *Hospitality Design,* October, 2015: 122-23.

"Platinum Circle." *Hospitality Design,* October, 2016: 120-121.

"Women of Influence." *Hospitality Design,* July 2010: 96.

This book is dedicated to

Maria A. Bentel FAIA & Dr. Frederick R. Bentel FAIA

Founding Partners of Bentel & Bentel Architects